A MOTHER GODDESS FOR

"Judith Lambert explores the appearances of Mary at Medjugorje and awakens within us the mysteries of the archetype of the mother goddess and its relationship to the Divine Mary—each of which generates a pilgrimage to sacred sites, grottoes, and healing springs not only to strengthen faith but to reinstate the indisputable fact that states of grace and miracles do exist in this world, even in dark times."

—Angeles Arrien, PhD
Cultural anthropologist and
author of *The Four-Fold Way* and *The Second Half of Life*

"In this well-written, heartfelt book, Judith Lambert shares her personal journey from skepticism to faith, while illuminating a greatly expanded view of the significance of the Virgin Mary. Although Mary has often been regarded merely as a supporting player in the historical story of Jesus, Lambert sees her as a living presence with a vital healing message for contemporary Christians and non-Christians alike. She shows us Mary the Mother Goddess who embodies the powerful, transformative, feminine energy that is so sorely needed to restore balance and harmony in a conflict-weary world. Reading this book feels like taking a long, refreshing drink from a sacred spring."

—Carolyn Godschild Miller, PhD
Author of *Creating Miracles*

"The Virgin Mary is indeed Christianity's adaptation of the archetypal Mother Goddess of prehistory, incorporating her compassionate nature and healing powers but rejecting her carnal nature and sexual being."

—Elinor W. Gadon, PhD
Resident Scholar, Brandeis University
Author of *The Once and Future Goddess*

"Embracing the feminine in today's hard-edged world requires ancient tools of questing. We travel to places of mystery. If we dare, the journey leads us to truths long buried. And we discover that dreamtime is a place as real as our own backyards. In *A Mother Goddess for Our Times*, the author generously shares her own quest and her own discoveries and provides a map we can all follow."

—Hal Zina Bennett, PhD
Author of *Writing Spiritual Books* and *Write From the Heart*

"If by 'chance' you are wondering if this book is for you, go for it. Whether you have a superficial interest in Mary as the divine feminine or feel a deep connection to her, you will not be disappointed. Judith Lambert takes us on a personal journey as an insightful teacher, an open-minded seeker, and a woman answering the deep call of feminine wisdom. I feel blessed that Mary comes into my life at important times to remind me what really matters. This book was one of those times for me."

—Terry Lynn Taylor
Author of *Messengers of Love, Light, and Grace*

"Judith Lambert invites us to open our hearts to the mysteries of the Divine Mary and find healing from the radiant light of feminine love. She celebrates and points the way to the ever-present goddess that inspires and blesses our lives."

—Bradford Keeney, PhD
Author of *Shaking Medicine, Bushman Shaman,* and *Shamanic Christianity*

A Mother Goddess for Our Times

Mary's Appearances at Medjugorje

JUDITH T. LAMBERT
Foreword by Margaret Starbird

ANN DURAN
PRODUCTIONS

Santa Fe, New Mexico

Published by: Ann Duran Productions
            1704B Llano Street #239
            Santa Fe, NM 87505

Editor: Ellen Kleiner
Glyph: Linda Mae Tratechaud
Book design and typography: Janice St. Marie
Cover design: Judith T. Lambert with Robert Pollock
Cover Painting: *The Hammam* by Omar El-Nagdi

Printed in the United States of America

Disclaimer: The author in no way encourages travel to Bosnia, which readers do at their own risk. Additionally, the names in this book have all been changed to protect the identity of individuals; any resemblance to persons living or dead is entirely coincidental.

Publisher's Cataloging-in-Publication Data
Lambert, Judith T.
A mother goddess for our times : Mary's appearances at Medjugorje / Judith T. Lambert. -- 1st ed. -- Santa Fe, N.M. : Ann Duran Productions, 2007.

   p. ; cm.
   ISBN-13: 978-0-9777083-0-7
   ISBN-10: 0-9777083-0-6
   Four separate pilgrimages to Medjugorje between 1986 and 1991 demonstrate to the author that daily sightings of the Virgin Mary can be interpreted as daily experiences of the universal feminine.
   Includes bibliographical references.

   1. Mother goddesses. 2. Goddess religion. 3. Mary, Blessed Virgin, Saint--Apparitions and miracles--Bosnia and Hercegovina--Medjugorje. 4. Women and religion. I. Title.

BT660.M44 L36 2007   2006921817
232.917/0949742--dc22   0705

10 9 8 7 6 5 4 3 2 1

To Her ~
who has given me everything

In gratitude . . .

I'd like to especially acknowledge Ellen Kleiner, whose various supportive roles as mentor and final editor were invaluable. I wish also to thank Naomi Rose for assistance in preparing the manuscript; Bill Roof for improving it; Marie Cantlon for her editorial advice; and Maria Collem, Colleen Lewis, and Richard Kenyon for their editorial services and support. I thank Janice St. Marie, Linda Mae Tratechaud, Robert Pollock, and Elizabeth Wolf for helping *Mother Goddess* move into the world. In addition, I would like to thank the many scholars whose work helped to reestablish the importance of feminine traditions. I am grateful to friends and family for their support, and I am immeasurably thankful to the most important people in my life—my daughter, Gabrielle, and my husband, John—without whom this book could not have been written.

Contents

Foreword

In September 1993, an X-ray of my daughter's right knee showed that her kneecap was in two distinct pieces, the source of acute tendonitis that was causing her leg to atrophy. For a freshman basketball player on an NCAA scholarship to Stanford University, this was the worst possible news. She called me in tears, sobbing that she would never play basketball again. Holding the telephone, listening to her disjointed narrative, I was stunned. When she had finished pouring out her heart, and after a moment to collect my own thoughts, I told her that I knew God had a plan for her life but I wasn't sure what it was. Her job was to try to fit into that plan—whatever it turned out to be. I told her to please ask all her friends to pray for her, and said I would ask mine to do the same. I tried to comfort her as best I could, even suggesting she might have to "red shirt" for a season to give her knee a chance to heal.

Three days later, in a semiwaking state, I received a vision—the only vision I've ever had. A beautiful lady, olive-skinned with long dark hair, dressed in a white sari and barefoot, was opening the door to my daughter's dormitory room. I could see my long, lean girl-child stretched out on her bed, wearing a dark red "Cardinal" T-shirt and beige Bermuda shorts. The lovely lady quietly knelt beside the bed, bent forward, and gently kissed my daughter's knee. Then she rose, looked at me, put her finger to her lips as if to say, "Don't disturb her!"—and silently tiptoed out of the room.

I knew I had seen the feminine face of God.

My twenty years of research and lecturing about the return of the sacred feminine was as nothing compared with the experience of her presence. She is here—often silent, but with us—the Lovely Lady who manifests in dreams and meditations, in shrines, sometimes in caves and grottoes, usually where there is darkness or cool running water. Typically the Beautiful Lady says nothing at all. When she does speak, she invariably asks us to pray—for peace, forgiveness, reconciliation, healing.

With increased consciousness, we become ever more aware that the external pilgrimage to sacred sites around the world is only a shadow of the inner pilgrimage, that amazing journey into the depths of our own psyches, where we ultimately encounter our Source. Concurrently we become acutely aware of the crying need in our time to connect with feminine aspects of divinity, those "waters" of spirit and truth that both purify and nurture our spiritual being. These waters are related to our tears, washing the windows of our souls. In connecting to our inner life and emotions, we experience tears of sorrow, yet also of joy and thanksgiving, long suppressed in a society that honors masculine attributes and devalues feminine ones. Ultimately, it is in reclaiming the sacred feminine as equal partner and Beloved that we will heal the parched wasteland of masculine hegemony.

In this book, Judith Lambert tells the story of her four pilgrimages to the Bosnian town of Medjugorje where, since 1980, Mary, the Blessed Mother of Jesus, has communicated with six young villagers and where many physical phenomena have attested to her presence. Lambert's outward journeys form the vehicle for the inward development of her spiritual awareness and gradual recognition of fundamental truths of spiritual growth, including longing for forgiveness and reconciliation in her personal relationships and for a deeper connection with the numinous presence of the sacred feminine.

Lambert presents valuable insight into the universal "goddess" archetype manifested in the Virgin Mary and the importance of connecting with the long-suppressed feminine aspects of the Divine. Her journey is a testament to the powerful way of the heart—accessing the Divine through experience, intuition, and direct emotional connection or "gnosis," thereby balancing the emphasis on rational thought, the preferred mode of the Western mind. Reunion with the "sacred feminine" archetype carries gifts of peace, joy, reconciliation, and integration of body, soul, and spirit on its wings.

This little book is a celebration of the journey of faith that reconnects us to feminine aspects of our Source—our journey into wholeness, which has the same root as "holiness." As we take that journey and reintegrate and cherish those aspects, we will begin to heal our families, our communities, and the world.

—Margaret Starbird
Steilacoom, Washington
May 1, 2007

Author's Note

Our planet is in dire need of rebalancing an excessively dominant masculine worldview, which seems to be why there is currently such an active resurgence of interest in the beliefs and traditions associated with ancient goddesses of various cultures. *A Mother Goddess for Our Times* explores the idea that female figures prominent in today's religions, particularly the Virgin Mary, can also be viewed as goddesses. The book investigates this idea from two perspectives—first, historical research on the attributes and functions of ancient goddesses in comparison to Mary, and second, insights resulting from personal encounters with the spiritual essence of Mary during pilgrimages to the town of Medjugorje, formerly in Yugoslavia and now in Bosnia, where six children had been having daily apparitions of the Virgin Mary. Now, more than twenty-six years since the apparitions began, the visionaries are adults and three still claim to see the Virgin daily. As a result of the reports of all six, together with numerous articles on the phenomenon and the fact that neither war nor disbelief has curtailed its occurrence, curiosity about the Mary visitations at Medjugorje is widespread.

This particular approach challenges preconceived notions about orthodox religion and simultaneously synthesizes qualities of goddess traditions and the universal feminine archetype, allowing us to see Mary within a broader continuum of historical and mythical female figures. Prior to my own theoretical, historical, and experiential explorations, if anyone suggested to me that the Virgin Mary should be viewed as a goddess whose functions were related to those of past pagan goddesses, I would have dismissed the idea as patently ridiculous. Today, however, I am convinced that she is the one goddess who can most vitally impact our lives and whose feminine essence can help correct the current imbalance globally.

Combining the term "mind-body healing" with Mary, a liberty occasionally taken in these pages, may be surprising to some readers, but here the term is meant to suggest a spiritual quest unconfined by dogma, which sometimes stifles spiritual growth. By combining mind-body viewpoints with fundamental truths of traditional religions, this book attempts to bridge the chasm between orthodox and nonorthodox factions rather than condemning either, and to promote tolerance for the views of all individuals and cultures in working toward increased understanding. Moreover, in addressing the feminine this book strives neither to disenfranchise men nor to further fracture the sexes, but rather to show how we can access feminine strengths that reside within both men and women.

My background as a student of metaphysics and comparative religion drove my investigations, both personal and historical. I grew up "between religious cracks," outside the confines of religious dogma and regular church attendance. As a result, I was free to pursue a variety of religious interests without prejudice and make my own determinations regarding spiritual knowledge. It was this quest for discovery that led me to embrace Marian influences and ultimately experience their profound gifts.

Setting Forth

In today's world, there seems to be an imbalance between masculine and feminine forces, resulting in patriarchal societies that perpetuate dominant male interpretations of phenomena, including aspects of culture and religion. This makes it difficult for many people to relate to orthodox religious beliefs and causes disharmony within and among various cultures. With the spiritual vision of the world now in question, the feminine face of God is being shown more obviously so that we may integrate the feminine aspect into our lives. Such an integration of masculine and feminine archetypal forces would result in a more balanced and unified consciousness, which in turn would foster greater enlightenment among cultures worldwide.

I have gained this realization through a twofold quest: study of the cultural functions of ancient and prehistoric goddesses and my own psychological and spiritual experiences during periodic visits to the tiny village of Medjugorje in Yugoslavia (now Bosnia), where many people have witnessed miracles and healings in connection with appearances of the Virgin Mary. For over twenty-six years now, people in this village claim to have seen her daily, including individuals who even as children are said to have regularly seen Mary, spoken to her, and received messages from her. Despite war and upheavals, the Marian visions and messages continue to this day. Before my visits, I had viewed the Virgin Mary as inseparable from the tradition of Christianity, especially the Roman Catholic Church, but my Medjugorje experiences have allowed me to see Mary in a much more universal, archetypal way, as a manifestation of the feminine spirit—a nurturer and mother figure with affinities to ancient goddesses and the mother-goddess of primitive cultures. A complete understanding of these experiences would not have been possible without the tandem study I undertook to uncover Mary's long history, highlights of which involved immersion in the published works of such scholars as Marina Warner, Merlin Stone, Elinor Gadon, Barbara G. Walker, and others knowledgeable in women's traditions.

Today, both inside and outside orthodox religion, people around the globe feel a need to get in touch with the universal feminine spirit, and at least 18 million people have made the pilgrimage to Medjugorje to experience Mary's apparitions and power. The miracles and healings that many of them have witnessed are extraordinary: rosaries turn to brilliant gold in front of their eyes, the sun spins in an unusual rhythm, the smell of roses occurs with no flowers in sight, and while visionary children see the Virgin Mary daily and receive messages from her, other pilgrims are inexplicably cured of their ailments. After making four visits to Medjugorje, each time experiencing directly the love and healing power of Mary, I can attest to the fact that my own being has been so radically changed and healed by the encounters that I have very new perceptions of life and a much greater understanding.

This book, for nontraditionalists and traditionalists alike, is intended to serve as a link between these sometimes divisive groups. Its purpose is to both share my personal experiences of the Virgin Mary and build a bridge between Mary and ancient goddesses, thereby showing how Mary can be seen as a universal figure of greater global significance than the church suggests and revealing her to be connected to earlier mother-goddesses, reflective of the archetypal feminine spirit who nurtures and loves all humanity. Throughout the book, I offer readers opportunities to know Mary for the first time as much more than the mother of Jesus—as in fact an embodiment of the powerful and healing force of the archetypal feminine spirit. It is my belief that considering the figure of Mary from the perspectives of intellectual inquiry and anecdotal reflections on my own experiences during my visits to Medjugorje will contribute to an understanding of Mary as a more universal goddess figure and a catalyst for love, peace, and enlightenment in our age.

As a nontraditionalist student of metaphysics and comparative religion and also teacher of dream work, I saw many deficiencies not only generally in orthodox religion but specifically in the renderings of Mary in church dogma, where she is portrayed as far less powerful than, and subordinate to, Jesus. Following my quest to comprehend the figure of Mary in a broader and more universal way, it became clear to me that the church's limited interpretation of Mary derives from prejudice about the role of women in a patriarchal society and that if we look to history and personal experience of miracles and healings occurring in present-day sanctuaries, it might be possible to see beyond these limited perspectives, recognize her as a universal goddess figure, and reclaim a more powerful sense of the feminine spiritual archetype within ourselves.

Further, my pilgrimages to Medjugorje convinced me that at certain sacred sites feminine energy is being intensified to accelerate transformational change by helping us rebalance the feminine and masculine energies and archetypes, and that the possibility exists for all of us to make such pilgrimages inwardly if not outwardly. I also hope that if we go on such a pilgrimage with an open mind and heart, we can come to see Mary's role as greater and more universal than the one assigned by patriarchal religion and view her instead as a figure symbolic of the feminine energy that can help rebalance us and lead to increased enlightenment.

Today, people believe that we can be free only by returning to attitudes about the earth, nature, and cultural cohesion characteristic of the mother-goddess devotion of primitive cultures or the goddess worship of ancient civilizations. We must keep in mind, however, especially regarding the later goddesses of Greece, that their images also were influenced by patriarchal cultures, as is reflected in stories about them. For example, Hera had an unfaithful husband and Persephone was raped, abducted to the underworld, and taken away from her mother and her own inheritance through male violence and dominance. Thus, in our investigations of these goddesses, as well as of Mary, we must take such cultural elements into account. Likewise, reclamation of our lost heritage, while a healing journey, requires us to experience some sadness as we recognize that the lives of women who went before us, including Mary, were often affected by the prejudices of patriarchal societies, resulting in stereotypical roles of madonna, seductress, or vessel for the birth of men of more significance. Yet we live in a time of unprecedented spiritual unfoldment. And while we cannot erase the past pain that women have endured, it is time for the universal feminine spirit to again ascend so that our wounds may be healed.

Medjugorje allowed me to directly experience the Divine beyond the confines of dogma. It is a sacred space in which natural laws as we know them are suspended and one enters a magical reality where the feminine spirit within us is energized to such an extent that deeper levels of the psyche can be transformed and we gain a more universal spiritual perspective. Thus, while I respect the truths inherent in all religious traditions, the more universal view of Mary revealed in this book has less to do with the Roman

Catholic Church or any other religious establishment than with transcendent, nondenominational energy.

The existence of the phenomena occurring at Medjugorje and similar places where Mary has appeared or is venerated, such as Lourdes, brings up many important questions to consider: Why does humankind still make pilgrimages to sites of feminine energy? What occurs beyond the human intellect that transforms the individual who is in touch with such feminine forces? By pondering these types of questions and allowing Mary's energy to fill our being, we can connect with the Divine within our own souls—and in doing so, reclaim the goddess in ourselves. The account that follows is an attempt to put the ineffable into words, to communicate the experiential and intellectual aspects of Mary as a universal mother-goddess figure imbued with the power to help heal and transform individuals, thereby opening the way for both personal and collective enlightenment.

CHAPTER ONE

A Pathway
to the Goddess

For the past two thousand years, the Virgin Mary has been etched in the minds of Westerners as an important religious figure. But like the veils that obscure her appearance in many images of her, Mary's true nature as a living goddess has been hidden. Indeed, she has been characterized as humble and meek. In descriptions of historical events, she appears insignificant except for her accomplishment of having given birth to Jesus. Once he is born, she essentially "fades into the woodwork," as author Marina Warner states, barely seen again until the Crucifixion. Then, as in Michelangelo's *Pieta*, she is depicted as a passive and sorrowful mourner holding her dead son in her arms. Religious tradition thus pictures her as existing to give birth to Jesus and bear his death, and apart from these functions having no impact or power.

The marginalization of Mary's true power and purpose parallels how women have been treated in our own culture. Many movies depict the limiting roles of women as either good and passive (the madonna) or bad and exciting (the seductress). Such narrow and polarized interpretations of women's roles in today's society are the result of distorted views of women projected by patriarchal societies over the centuries, all of which mirrored the religious symbols and archetypes of their time. With the marginalized image of Mary as a present-day role model, women, whether they are Catholic or not, have grown up accepting the limitation of feminine power and the destructive legacy of the madonna-or-seductress role choice.

Increasingly, however, women are now refusing to accept this polarization, realizing they can be sexual *and* nurturing, passionate *and* compassionate, powerful because of who they are rather than how they dominate or allow themselves to be dominated. In seeking their true essence, women have found inspiring role models in various goddesses of antiquity and in the earlier mother-goddess traditions of primitive societies, associated with fertility, earth, and nature. In response to groundbreaking scholarship and archaeo-logical discoveries, there has been a resurgence of respect for the feminine aspect of God as reflected in such goddesses. From the mother-goddess of primitive cultures to the Sumerian Inanna, the Egyptian Isis, the Greek Demeter, the Indian Lakshmi, the Japanese Amaterasu, and the Tibetan Tara, goddesses of the past are now being invoked through rituals, prayers, and images.

Transcending the predefined roles of women can be regarded as a positive development, since for our modern world to gain balance a great infusion of feminine spiritual energy is required to offset the prevailing standards. Resurrected goddess worship, however, is associated with other cultures and times; and while these figures had a profound impact on the people who visited their shrines and attended rituals in their honor, contemporary Westerners often have difficulty relating to them. For example, it is not easy to imagine Nut, the Egyptian sky goddess linking heaven and earth with her arching body. Ultimately, although we may identify intellectually with goddesses of other cultures and times, we tend to experience the feminine aspect of God with greater immediacy and profundity while contemplating a figure more reflective of our own cultural heritage—a function the Virgin Mary can fulfill.

Whether Catholic, Protestant, Jewish, nondenominational, or interdenominational, for over two thousand years people from many Western cultures have identified with Mary as a representative of feminine spirituality, despite the limited power and attention accorded her by patriarchal perspectives. Now, especially, her power seems to be increasingly prevalent at various centers, such as Lourdes and Medjugorje, where Mary is said to have appeared, given messages, and effected healings, offering people possibilities for a direct experience of her energy in lieu of the indirect understanding provided by religious texts and rituals. These towns and others have become pilgrimage sites for millions seeking the love and healing of a universal feminine spirit.

For our consciousness to be transformed by this type of encounter, we must surrender rationality; allow Mary to speak to us in her own language of emotions, images, and miracles; and accept the guidance that emerges from this intuitive experience of the Divine. As an example of such encounters and as an inspiration for others to consider such a quest, I am revealing my own experiences with the feminine divine spirit of Mary at Medjugorje.

CHAPTER TWO

A Goddess among Us

First Pilgrimage to Medjugorje

My own experience with the transformative energy of Mary during visits to Medjugorje began serendipitously, while I was teaching dream interpretation to a group of Catholic women in a remote area of Saudi Arabia who told me about the miraculous events they had witnessed in Medjugorje. I was young and living in what seemed like a Peace Corps outpost in the coastal Eastern Province. There were few TVs and only one local channel, which beamed censored information during off-work hours. The Internet had not yet been invented; our phone calls to the States had to be booked two days in advance. In short, the global village was yet a dream.

The town of Medjugorje, in Yugoslavia at the time, had for five years been the site of daily visits from Mother Mary and therefore was considered a sanctuary of the feminine and place for accessing personal strength and a sense of the miraculous. "The sun spins and pulsates in the sky," one woman told me. "And you can look at it for hours without hurting your eyes."

"Incredible healings happen there," insisted another woman. "Parents carry their crippled children up a rocky mountain, and soon after, the children can walk up on their own. It's like Lourdes!"

"Rosaries mysteriously change color there. Mine went from silver to gold," a woman named Elena exclaimed. "I've seen others turn pink, copper, or rose-gold. Some even go back and forth. Why don't you have dinner with me and let me tell you more."

I silently wondered what was wrong with these women. Their assertions made no sense to me. And while I knew nothing about Medjugorje, as a longtime student of metaphysics and a graduate student in religious studies, I had indeed heard of miraculous shrines and considered the stories about them absurd. Curious to test my long-held beliefs, I accepted the invitation.

Later, as we sat over coffee and dessert in Elena's suburban dining room, I asked her to describe her view of what was really going on in Medjugorje.

"Six children called visionaries can see and even touch a three-dimensional lady they claim is the Virgin Mary. They are the only people who see these apparitions, although millions of individuals from all over the world have come there since the phenomenon first began in 1981. The six children are Vitzka, Mariana, Ivan, Jacov, Ivanka, and Maria. Jacov was only six or seven when Mary first appeared to him. The others were not more than fifteen. Ivan's about twenty-five now. Two of the children—Ivanka and Mariana—have received all the secrets, so they do not see her anymore, except on their birthdays and other special occasions. The other four still see Our Lady on both hills, in the church, and in their homes."

The only thing I could compare this to were the oracular shrines of antiquity, the most renowned of which was at Delphi in Greece. Might Medjugorje be functioning in the same manner?

I wondered. "Where did the children start seeing these visions?" I asked out loud.

"The first one occurred on top of a hill, and then they showed up on top of a steep mountain, where the children have put up a cross," Elena replied. "Mary still appears to them there or in their homes, but mostly she's seen inside the church. Millions of people have been transformed by her presence even though they can't see her apparitions. Another mysterious thing is how the church was built where some apparitions now appear. Twenty years ago the villagers built the church five times bigger than was needed to accommodate the town's three or four hundred residents. They said they didn't know why, that they were somehow compelled to keep on building. Then years later, when the apparitions began occurring, eighteen million people streamed in from all over the world, too many for the church to hold at one time. 'Our Lady had plans' is how they now explain the building of the church."

"And what is Mary's purpose in appearing?" I asked, fascinated yet still wondering how Elena had come to believe all this stuff.

She shook her head. "Only the children really know. They've each been given ten secrets they can't reveal, about events happening in the earth's future. It is believed that Mary predicted certain earthquakes and wars that have already come to pass. And it seems her messages are meant to save us, for her words are always of peace. 'I am the Blessed Virgin, the Queen of Peace' is how she announced herself to the children when they first saw her on Apparition Hill, wearing a crown and cape of stars above her long dark veiled hair and standing on a bed of clouds."

I could not explain the strange excitement that caught hold of me despite the fact that I had no clear sense of what had been happening in Medjugorje or what it might have to do with me. Although Elena's stories sounded preposterous to me, I thought back to my studies of goddesses in ancient cultures and parallels immediately sprang to mind. Isis, too, had worn a cape with glittering stars embroidered on the surface, and stars had crowned the head of Venus. In representing the figure of Mary, I mused, had the early church incorporated symbols related to goddesses of earlier cultures?

Elena's words mysteriously stirred old longings in me. Yet I was at a loss to comprehend just how a figure as traditional as the Virgin Mary fit with my radically nontraditional beliefs as a social outcast, political dissident, and adherent of shamanic lifeways. This made me wonder if the stories about apparitions of Mary were affecting me on an unconscious archetypal level and if something of universal significance was unfolding within me. Having been to channelers, healers, and tarot and palm readers, as well as having studied esoteric traditions and become a teacher of dream analysis, I asked myself, could I also be open to exploring the phenomena occurring at Medjugorje?

While I sat listening to Elena, conflicting thoughts ran through my mind. Were these children deluded? If they indeed had been chosen to receive spiritual messages for the world, were they human channelers?

As if she had read my thoughts, Elena assured me, "The children at Medjugorje have all been psychoanalyzed and subjected to tests to determine whether they are lying, and even the greatest skeptics had to admit that they are not." Then she asked suddenly, "Do you want to see my rosary?"

After I nodded with anticipation, she went into her bedroom and returned holding the glinting family rosary. "It was sterling silver before I went to Medjugorje, and now you can see where it's turned gold," she revealed.

The beads, cross, and medallion with Mary's image lay draped against the pink of Elena's palm. Where it curved against her wrist, the rosary was silver, but lower down, toward her fingers, the color bled into gold, while the lowest part of the beads, cross, and medallion were all gold.

"That's remarkable," I exclaimed, touching the place where the color had changed. "How did it happen?" I asked in continued disbelief.

"I prayed, and one day I felt my heart become lighter. That's when the rosary turned gold," Elena said.

Even though I'd always been a spiritual seeker, I found it difficult to simply surrender to mysteries without being able to comprehend events with my intellect. Being also a skeptic, I could see how the apparitions at Medjugorje would be dismissed as wishful thinking or collective brainwashing. And yet, since I accepted the mind's ability to influence matter, I decided that the events at Medjugorje could conceivably be explained by this phenomenon in addition to faith and group prayer. I then considered the possibility that magical events which had presumably occurred at pagan shrines resembled the miracles at Medjugorje, since these too involved invocations, sacred artifacts, and ritual acts. Weren't *magic* and *miracle* merely different words expressing the same phenomenon? I wondered. Finally, I concluded that while science might explain some of Elena's reports as collective brainwashing or the power of mind over matter, if people were healed or the color of their rosaries changed, ultimately it did not matter how it came about so much as that it testified to the existence of unseen forces that could influence our reality positively.

Before I left Elena's house, she suggested I go to Medjugorje and see for myself what was happening, a possibility that at first seemed farfetched to me. Unable to make sense of Elena's stories, I wondered how I would ever come to terms with them. Yet this encounter with her prompted me to continue questioning and pursuing any leads that might shed more light on the events she described.

My inquiries about these spiritual events stemmed, in part, from the fact that I lacked a traditional religious education but nevertheless was spiritually inclined and had an ongoing need for spiritual nourishment. Due to my lack of formal religious training, I was free to follow my own spiritual path and learn about many religious traditions. My studies, however, had been intellectual endeavors, and I now felt the need to seek more direct spiritual experience to see if it would help fill a void in my life and lead to greater enlightenment.

While reviewing my past spiritual pursuits, I suddenly remembered a religious experience I'd had long before. One day when I was about thirteen, I watched a movie on TV called *The Song of Bernadette*, starring Jennifer Jones, in which a girl was visited by Mary, an event that made her face radiant with love and joy. I recalled how I had longed to have such an experience and said out loud, "I would do *anything* to see Mary and feel such love and joy."

Now I realized more fully that all the women I had spoken with about Medjugorje had had such an experience, as was evident if only from their sense of wonder. Clearly, something powerful going on at Medjugorje was beyond explanation, and indeed, beyond words. Although the women had tried to describe their visits as having made them feel "more peaceful," "taken care of," or "no longer troubled by things that used to cause despair," the difficulty they had articulating their intangible feelings increased my desire to better understand their experiences.

Finally, after overriding some of my conflicts about the reports I'd heard, I conceded that if at Medjugorje the sun spun and earth-changing prophecies came out of the mouths of children, I should not deny myself the possibility of feeling the radiance of the girl I had seen in the movie during my childhood. This decision to go to Medjugorje to see what spiritual events might be happening was a major turning point in my quest to increase my spiritual understanding. But still I viewed the pilgrimage from an outsider's vantage point—like a spiritual anthropologist. I had no idea that my life was about to be irreversibly transformed.

Pilgrimage sites associated with the veneration of Mary, such as Lourdes and Medjugorje, have a magnetic allure for religious people who long for a direct spiritual experience. Not being a religious person, in anticipation of my journey to Medjugorje I prepared by periodically engaging in prayer and meditation, believing it would maximize my mind's ability to receive the power of any spiritual energy I might encounter. I also focused on interpreting my dreams as a means for gaining psychological insights and self-knowledge. Dreams, I believed, have residual effects on the psyche, similar to actual memories, and the remarkable ones can be recalled to offer direction in life. Dream interpretation, like an intuitive hunch, is a feminine way of perceiving that has been used as a form of guidance throughout history, as is evidenced in the prophetic dreams found in the Old and New Testaments and the dreams incubated through rituals by devotees of the goddess Isis so she would come to heal them. Aware that dreams can direct spiritual growth, I invited mine to become a primary source for guidance during my time at Medjugorje, which would be tantamount to receiving the wisdom of an inner goddess.

Two months before I was to embark on my ten-day pilgrimage, I had my first of many dreams about Medjugorje, a deeply satisfying confirmation of my plans:

> I am in a group of people going to see the visionaries
> in Medjugorje. I get the feeling that we are going to

be robbed, so I try to hide my diamond watch. Then I decide to follow my intuition and leave. As I look back, the others are being robbed. I hide my valuables and try to see the visionaries by myself.

I am now outside, amidst old ruins. I try to stand on them, but they crumble under my feet and I slide to the ground. As I regain my balance and look up, I notice the vision has started. A blue-white beam of light comes down from the sky into a house so powerfully I can't keep my eyes open. I ask my husband, John, who is now standing next to me, if he can feel it too. He says yes. I just want to feel the powerful energy.

I woke up from this dream inspired about my impending trip to Medjugorje, as it seemed to predict that I would have some revelatory experience there. The first half of the dream appeared to represent the physical reality of my life, which had become excessively materialistic, obstructing any connection I might have with spiritual realities. The necessity of hiding my diamond watch was symbolic of the need to protect myself from being robbed of something valuable, perhaps my inner spiritual life.

Seventeen days later I had another dream:

I am in my childhood room, lying in bed. I look up and see the Virgin Mary in the air, transparent and delineated only by a white outline. I am awestruck. All of a sudden my entire brain glows white, and I am healed.

I awoke from this dream feeling cleansed of a psychological turmoil that had been troubling me since as far back as I could remember. Adopted at a young age, I suffered immeasurably from the loss of my biological mother, and, although I was cared for, the emotional scars from this early trauma left me with uncontrollable mood swings, abandonment issues, low self-esteem, little joy in life, and a pervasive sense of dread. A glum, if not tragic, person, I had struggled to stay content, and now this appearance of the Virgin Mary in my dream suggested that a universal feminine force was about to become more tangible in my day-to-day reality.

These two dreams indeed foreshadowed future events. Soon after the second one, I joined a small group of Catholic women from the United States who were preparing to embark on a pilgrimage to Medjugorje, where my life was about to change radically, as the following narrative reveals.

March 15, 1989

We arrived in Dubrovnik and, during the three-hour taxi ride to Medjugorje, talked about everything from religion and the meaning of life to our expectations regarding the next few days. Some of the women spoke excitedly about the prospect of seeing the Virgin Mary, but another dashed their hopes, saying, "The children are the only ones who actually see her. The rest of us have to depend on faith. Even so, pilgrims are convinced that she is appearing because of the love and peace they feel, the healing they have received, or the miracles they attribute to her presence."

As we entered the village of Medjugorje, the driver gestured toward two hills, one small and one large. "There is Mount Krizevac," he said, pronouncing it "Kreezsh-a-vix" and pointing toward the larger hill, which had a big cross on top. "That is where Our Lady often appears in a special nighttime apparition to the visionary named Ivan." Although I had heard of this before, actually being here made me wonder if it was an illusion and if the villagers had perhaps lost their sanity and bought into a huge lie. As I stared at the steep mountain outlined against the black sky, suddenly it seemed to light up. "Oh look," I cried, "the cross is radiating light!"

No one else saw it, and when I looked again I didn't either. Have I lost my marbles? I asked myself. Feeling a little foolish, I wondered how I'd become so irrational, then figured I'd simply been primed for seeing miracles, having listened to so many stories rendered about them with great conviction.

Exhilarated and exhausted, we arrived at the homestead of Lidija, the matron who was to be our host. After tumbling out of the taxi like expectant children, we carried our bags to a series of rooms over a converted barn that was to be our place of residence until the pilgrims staying in the main house had left. I missed my husband John, but knew I'd keep busy until his arrival five days later. Once settled, our group fell asleep to the scent of composting hay and the sounds of cows lowing into the night.

March 16

Our first morning in Medjugorje began early, with breakfast and a regional history lesson presented by Lidija's son, Martin. Located in a valley nestled between two mountains, with the church at its center, this simple old-world farming community is a bustling Mecca for pilgrims from all over the world. Since the apparitions began, there has been considerable growth, with cafés, restaurants, curio shops selling religious articles, hotels, and new chalet-style homes springing up all around town to accommodate the visitors. The single main street leads to a roundabout that forks into three roads—one heading toward the center of town and the other two passing by vineyards and villagers' homes before climbing Mount Krizevac and the small mountain known as Podbrdo Hill.

By now I was impatient to meet the visionaries and stand on the spot where Mary had appeared. Martin drove me into town for the daily 10:00 a.m. Mass in English, given by the American priest who lives in Medjugorje year round. The service was uneventful other than the sense of an English-speaking community it offered in this place so far from home.

In the afternoon, I went to meet two of the visionaries, Vitzka and Ivan, with my roommate, Karen, who had already made two visits to Medjugorje. As we walked toward the visionaries' houses at the base of the smaller mountain, Karen told me she had experienced profound healing the first time she had come. When we arrived at Vitzka's house, I was very moved by this young, dark-haired woman, who has a sweet grin, shy eyes, and radiates happiness through her countenance.

Afterward, we climbed up nearby Podbrdo Hill, also called Apparition Hill because it was there, in June of 1981, that the visionaries first saw the beautiful numinous lady who introduced herself as the "Queen of Peace." From the conversations I over-heard during my twenty-minute climb up the hard stone path, it was clear that most pilgrims believe "Our Lady" is appearing to heal people and encourage peace.

While climbing, I realized that feminine deities throughout history had been given epithets similar to Mary's. For example, "Queen of Heaven" was used for pagan goddesses such as Inanna, Ishtar, Astarte, Aphrodite, Diana (Artemis), Hathor, and Juno; the church declared Mary "Queen of Heaven" shortly after its official 1950 announcement of her assumption into heaven. Other names for Mary that were first used in connection with ancient goddesses include Blessed Virgin, Mother of God, Our Lady, Ever-Virgin, Most Holy One, Glorious One, Empress of Hell, Lady of All the World, Bride of God, and Mother Goddess. By contrast, variations of the name Mary were often applied to pagan forerunners of the Virgin, such as Marratu, Marah, Mariham, Marian, Miriam, Marianne,

Myrrhine, Maria, Marina, Aphrodite-Mari, and the Syrian goddess Astarte's epithet "Mother Mari." Not surprisingly, Mary's mother's name, Anne, was applied also to goddesses of antiquity.

At the top of the mountain, I could see a panoramic view of the valley, with its patchwork of greens and browns. I sat under a gray stone cross that had been erected on the spot where Mary first appeared, which was now piled high with flowers, votary candles, and prayer petitions. It was the ground itself, however, which provided the most convincing evidence that something magical had happened here, for its energy felt immediately comforting. I prayed for a long time before returning.

At 3:00 p.m., Karen and I went to a lecture given by an English-speaking priest, followed at 4:00 p.m. by a Croatian rosary service at the huge stone church, which was crowded with hundreds of people reciting the rosary in fourteen different languages. The swell of sound was both mesmerizing and confusing. Not having a rosary and unfamiliar with the ritual, I understood little other than "Hail, Holy Queen, Mother of Mercy, Our Life, Our Sweetness, and Our Hope," though I was happy meditating along with the prayers and absorbing the positive energy of the pilgrims.

The daily evening apparition at the church occurs at 5:40. I was hoping, however, for a mountaintop display, since there is something thrilling about encountering a spiritual presence in the open air, unconfined by a physical structure or religious paraphernalia. It turns out that night apparitions occur on the hilltop about twice a week but the Catholic Church has never officially recognized these visions and the government even jailed a priest, Father Jozo Zovko, for protecting the children who attended them. The children would kneel in front of the outdoor altar, and as they prayed, their eyes would converge on a single spot, as if they all saw the same thing at the same time.

Despite my preference for an open-air experience, I attended the apparition at the church. Awed by the uplifting energy there, I stayed for Mass.

I have been here only one day and am already permeated with light. I feel an undeniable promise of miracles to come.

March 17

I am getting used to the crowds of all nationalities walking the streets and browsing through the curio shops piled high with religious objects for sale. The people's faces have none of that grim, exhausted look typical of tourists, but instead reflect an inner energy. Since we are all pilgrims, conversations revolve around our spiritual lives. Stories of miracles are traded like ordinary news, and I feel left out since I have not yet had a dramatic experience. Still, the sense of wonder here is palpable, and I feel like a child at Disneyland for the first time.

After lunch, Karen and I climbed back up Podbrdo Hill, where I again sat under the cross meditating and praying. This time I reflected on my childhood and how my adopted parents, both alcoholics, had been oblivious to its effects on family life. "Mary," I called out silently, feeling the still-embedded pain of my youth, "help me." Abruptly I sank into a state of relaxation in which all that mattered was the peace and love that exuded from the ground into my body. Exalted yet humbled, I could feel an infinitely loving energy enter me and simultaneously enfold me in its arms, like the mother I hungered for.

When I opened my eyes, I saw a group of people nearby praying over someone. Approaching the leader, I asked her to pray over me too.

"What is your problem?" she asked.

I told her of my childhood memories and various problems I

was having with money and relationships. She questioned me a bit, nodded, then placed her hands on my head.

Suddenly an agonizing cry erupted from deep within me, like that of a wounded animal searching for shelter. I felt a stab of pain in my heart, after which an unexpected sense of guilt kept me sobbing. It was as if I were on a teeter-totter with someone bigger and heavier sitting at the other end, causing me to express hidden emotions so uncontrollably that it shocked me. After about twenty minutes, the torrent of grief gradually subsided, leaving me visibly shaken.

Unburdened of the intensity, I became deeply aware of my surroundings. And now embarrassed by my lack of control, I asked Karen not to tell anyone about this sudden and inexplicable occurrence.

"Don't worry," she said kindly. "Things like this often happen in Medjugorje."

March 18

Some of the women in our group are becoming argumentative with one other, and after the profundity of yesterday's experience I find their pettiness difficult to endure and have decided to pursue my spiritual life on my own. In light of this, my dream about hiding the diamond watch so it wouldn't be stolen seems prophetic: several of us are being robbed of our valuable experiences here by the negativity in our midst. My dream also indicated I would meet up with my husband to have a profound encounter with divine energy, and indeed today John left the United States for Medjugorje.

At 3:00 p.m. I sat against the wall of the gray stone church, its two huge towers stark against the background of the mountains. In the small park area, roped off and planted with grass and flowers, stands a tall white stone statue of Mary with graceful outstretched arms bearing rosaries that had been placed across her fingers by supplicants. While waiting, I contemplated the distinctly different forms the image of the Virgin Mary takes on in various cultures. Whereas this statue of Mary is slender, white, and pure looking, elsewhere I've seen images of Mary as a dark-haired and dark-complexioned earthy woman, some resembling Polynesian women with loose, flowing hair and a baby at the breast. Being here with people of so many nationalities, I am becoming more aware of how Mary seems to mirror various cultures at least as much as she influences them. Mirroring a culture that worships them, I imagine, might endow any female deity with the power to keep the world in better balance by encouraging equal status between women and men in every way possible.

When John arrived, I ran joyfully to meet him. We prayed at the church, and over dinner talked of my time here. Later, we carried my things into the main house, where there was now space for us. Leaving the bickering atmosphere of the barn and having my husband by my side, I felt settled.

March 19

The day began bright and beautiful as we walked through the grapevine-lined fields to church. In the afternoon, we climbed Podbrdo with Karen and Wendy, another woman from the group, to pray instead of going to the late-afternoon rosary and apparition at the church. At about 4:00 p.m., I noticed John staring intently at the sun with an expression of awe on his crimson-washed face. Although I had heard about the sun's spinning and pulsing with radiant colors, I had been afraid to look at it; but now, with John's encouragement, I too saw it spin and pulsate like a lighted pinwheel, its center covered as in a solar eclipse. Together we stared directly into the golden sun for about half an hour, until it set.

Astonished by the scene we had witnessed, I recalled references from virtually all major religions about mysterious activity of the sun signifying manifestations of the Divine. For example, the Old Testament tells how Joshua was able to stop the sun from moving along its path, while the New Testament reports that there was no sun at Jesus's Crucifixion. I'm beginning to think that here in Medjugorje the sun dances to a divine plan and that we are at a sacred site.

At night I had another revealing dream:

> I go to a jewelry store and ask to trade in my diamond watch for a bracelet. The replacement I am given, with one exquisite and very shiny diamond, turns to thick wood on my arm. I am overjoyed and never want to give it back.

It seems that now I have exchanged my materialism for values that are more authentic and spiritual, represented by the single diamond suggestive of divine light. I interpret this dream, in tandem with my surprising sense of contentment here, to mean that I am progressing in my spiritual quest.

March 20

People who went to Podbrdo last night saw the luminous figure of the Virgin walking for about fifteen minutes under the cross on top of Mount Krizevac after Ivan had his apparition. Contrary to the general belief that only the visionaries can see the Virgin, it seems in rare instances pilgrims also get to glimpse her. I look forward to joining the pilgrims as they climb Mount Krizevac tonight.

As it turned out, the walk by candlelight and flashlight took about an hour. The path, like the one to Podbrdo, is formed completely of stone and dirt but is much steeper. Each step was an effort as we moved slowly forward by sheer willpower. At the top, we gathered around Ivan, while he stood by the cross viewing the night's apparition. As far as I know, no one saw it but him.

March 21

Since Easter is approaching, John and I decided to go back up to Mount Krizevac during daylight hours to visit the Stations of the Cross, a Catholic procession encompassing the events of Jesus's life from his arrest to his Resurrection. There is a rumor that the crucifix at the eleventh station is bleeding. The small crucifix was placed there several years ago by a pilgrim who had been healed of blindness while in Medjugorje.

When we reached the eleventh station, we saw that the crucifix was constructed of wood, with the body of Jesus made of beige plastic. While there was no active bleeding, I could see what appeared to be blood on the rocks below and blood stains around the crown of thorns on the figure's head and under the arms. The idea of bleeding crucifixes doesn't move me in the same way as a spinning, pulsating sun, perhaps because I realize, from my studies in comparative religion, that this sort of phenomenon is relatively common and might even be rigged. History is rife with reports of bleeding crucifixes, weeping statues or images, and individuals developing stigmata on parts of their bodies. Some people attribute these phenomena to the psychokinetic power of the people involved, who created the manifestations through the sheer energy of their minds. To me, however, while I have no doubt the mind can influence matter, the phenomena occurring at Medjugorje are beyond the grasp of the rational mind and often scientifically unexplainable.

At the top of Mount Krizevac there is a large cement cross put up by the villagers about fifty years ago, and since Mary's message to the children suggested the benefits of praying beneath this particular cross, I prayed for a long time. While descending Mount Krizevac, it became clear that in the few days since my arrival I had begun feeling better about my life.

Back at the house, pilgrims returning from a bus trip related an incredible story about the bus being mysteriously infused with the scent of roses, reminiscent of the "odor of sanctity" that sometimes surrounds saints and holy people and is said to awaken the senses and elevate consciousness. "The whole bus smelled of roses," they reported nonchalantly, as if saying, "Today we ate breakfast." Could I, should I, believe what they are saying? I asked myself.

I was on fire, and if it was true I wanted to smell it myself. Reflecting on the flowers and scents associated with Mary—such as the rose, lily, and myrrh—I recalled most have been consistently associated with figures representative of the feminine spirit from pagan times until the present. In fact, the sense of smell has historically been an avenue to a heightened spirituality and thought to affect dreams. The olfactory gland, responsible for the sense of smell, is considered the most sensitive sense organ and is extremely acute during sleep. Odors are also said to stimulate the pituitary gland, the master gland of the body, associated with spiritual attunement. The theory behind the age-old tradition of burning incense during meditation is that the odor will stimulate the pituitary gland to alter consciousness, an outcome similar to the odor of sanctity's impact on an individual.

The association of odors and certain flowers with saints and spirituality, as appropriated by the Catholic Church, lies deep in history. The idea of an odor of sanctity itself can be traced back to embalming and mummification practices in ancient Egypt, a ritual performed by the jackal god Anubis to prepare a corpse for passage to the afterworld. The Christians, later applying this idea to their saints, said they had died in the odor of sanctity, assuring followers of their immortality. The perfume of heaven, exuding from the remains of saints or sometimes surrounding living holy personages, was believed to produce miracles in those who could smell it.

Of the flowers and scents associated with Mary, the rose, previously regarded as the flower of Venus, was perhaps the most well-known. In addition to Venus, the goddess Cybele was garlanded with roses; and in India, the Great Mother was addressed as the Holy Rose. Upon transferring this symbolic flower to the Virgin Mary, Christianity conferred upon her the name Holy Rose, as well as Rosebush, Rosegarland, Rosegarden, Mystic Rose, and Queen of the Most Holy Rosary.

Similarly, the lily's link to Mary had prior associations. It was connected with the Sumerian-Babylonian goddess Lilith, the Great Mother; the Phoenician goddess Astarte, prototype of Mary; and the Roman goddesses Juno, Hera, and Venus. The lily often represented the virgin aspect of a goddess, while the rose represented the maternal.

The scent of myrrh, also originating in earlier forms of worship, represented both the life-giving and life-taking aspects of the tripartite goddess, typically referred to as the crone aspect. Significantly, weeping icons of the Virgin are from time to time reported to shed tears of myrrh, which are perhaps rigged.

The fact that all these scents and symbols now connected with Mary were first associated with early goddesses points to the idea of a universal feminine principle, or archetype, of which Mary is only one representative. This realization inspires me to explore more such parallels.

March 22

I've finally decided to experience confession—primarily because Mary apparently has said here in Medjugorje that monthly confessions are helpful. I had ambivalent feelings about this decision because I view confession as a man-made ritual, not something divinely inspired. And I had never felt a strong urge to confess, though like most people I have felt guilty about certain thoughts and actions. Nevertheless, since the intent to purify the self is of great importance in a spiritual quest, I figured confession could function both symbolically and experientially, so I went into the church and did it. After confession, I stepped out into the daylight and indeed felt freer, highly aware, and more compassionate toward the people sitting against the church's walls, their eyes focused inward in contemplation.

Now I can say that while it is not necessary to go to church to have such an experience—and indeed, I probaby won't go again—for those who function better with more traditional structure than I prefer, confession can in fact serve as a stimulus for growth. I've concluded that any ritual is only as effective as the intent of the participant, meaning that rituals involving goddesses of the past must therefore be as beneficial physically and spiritually as today's church rituals.

March 23

John and I traveled forty miles to visit Father Jozo Zovko, who spent eighteen months in jail in Ljubuski and is banned from living in Medjugorje. The reason for the prohibition is that he helped the visionary children at the onset of the apparitions. He reportedly has also seen the Virgin Mary in an apparition.

After giving a sermon at his church in Ljubuski, he said to us through a translator, "You must continue to convert your hearts to God." I understood this not to mean that we should convert to Catholicism, the religion I assumed was already predominant here, but rather that we should move away from earthly desires and negative thoughts, toward our spiritual home. That people who are already Catholic are being told to convert underscores Mary's message that true conversion requires an inner development that has nothing to do with one's professed religion. I thought how wonderful it would be—and how likely to increase tolerance worldwide—if humanity realized that it is an individual's responsibility to transform their heart, not their denomination or religion, and that this alone represents the quintessence of spirituality.

March 24

After returning from Ljubuski yesterday, I witnessed the change in color of a rosary! Lanore, one of the ladies in the group, has a sterling silver rosary that turned gold, except for two beads, which are still silver. I was startled to see this phenomenon and still can't fathom it. What in the world is going on here? I asked myself.

Since then I've been looking more closely at people's rosaries. The traditional one has a crucifix trailing below a central medallion that usually contains a picture of the Virgin. On some of the central medallions, the picture of Mary has changed in color around the heart. In others, the rays of the heart in the medallion have turned pink, rose-gold, copper, or even all three shades. Sometimes the colors change back and forth—rapidly overnight or slowly over a number of days. One young woman's rosary hasn't changed, but a circular pink burst now covers a large area on the back of her crucifix; when she showed me this, her radiant face indicated that she had experienced a corresponding burst of love.

As a result of studying many rosaries, I'm beginning to understand that the changes each one has undergone reflects its owner's inner transformations. Some people change slowly because they need to learn patience, while others transform quickly, perhaps to bolster their faith. It seems that something beyond religion is taking place here—some kind of inner alchemical shift that causes rosaries to change materially.

In an effort to better comprehend this cause and effect, I asked a girl, "How did it happen for you?"

She looked up with bright, peaceful eyes and answered, "I was praying with my heart."

March 25

Today, we spent the rosary time outside the church so that during the apparition we could watch the sun spin, an event that continually reconfirms the inner change I feel. Podbrdo is where I sense Mary's presence the strongest and where my meditations seem to result in the most healing. I love the vista of the fertile basin below me, the clear blue spring sky, and the dozen beautiful roses that have been placed on the cross in honor of Our Lady's appearances.

Like the early mother-goddess figures associated with fertility and the earth, in this place Mary also is venerated in natural surroundings. In addition to Medjugorje, many other Catholic places of visitation are outdoors, such as shrines to Our Lady of Guadeloupe, Mexico; Our Lady of Lourdes, France; and Our Lady of Fatima, Portugal. The grove and garden themselves originally symbolized the body of the mother-goddess, who was connected with the earth and fertility. Later, Eve lived in a garden, and Mary's often in one. Although these gardens are supposed to represent Mary's virginity, I wonder if there's also a hidden connection here to the mother-goddess figures of primitive cultures.

Along with the grove and garden, specific plants have long been associated with the feminine essence. Traditionally, ancient goddesses were worshipped as guardians of the crops and promoters of fertility and the harvest. Many common plants originally connected to pagan goddesses were later linked to Mary, such as corn and wheat, symbols of the goddess Demeter. At Medjugorje, Mary's messages directly address the harvest and other labors of the field, likewise echoing the functions of earlier goddesses.

Apparitions of Mary have also been affirmed by natural signs, especially holy springs both in Medjugorje and other pilgrimage sites. For example, during an apparition of Our Lady on Mount Krizevac, she promised the children she would leave "a sign from heaven so no one will be able to dispute" her visitation. There is speculation that the sign will be a spring or a rainbow; presently, however, the apparitions themselves are still occurring. At the place of Mary's visitation in Lourdes, there appeared a spring whose miraculous curative powers continue to be reported today. Similarly, the goddess Diana made a holy spring in Rome, one so revered that today it is sometimes considered the Lourdes of the Roman Empire. So it seems that holy springs found in conjunction with Marian veneration offer yet another parallel with circumstances surrounding the worship of early goddesses. Such symbolism reflects the healing given to humanity from the Divine.

March 26
While back up on Podbrdo Hill this afternoon, John and I saw that the beautiful roses left there yesterday remained unwilted—another miracle, we thought, until a woman who had hiked up with us touched them and discovered they were not real. Feeling embarrassed, we laughed heartily at our mistake, realizing how gullible we had become in expecting miracles at every turn in Medjugorje.

As John and I came down from Podbrdo and rounded the corner near the visionary Vitzka's house, we found her outside alone. "Will you give us a blessing?" we asked, and she placed her hands on top of our heads for nearly a minute. We felt fortunate to be touched by someone close to Mary. Gullible or not, so strengthened am I, both physically and mentally, that I never want to leave this place.

March 27
John departed this morning, and I have only two more days here myself. I've moved into a room at Lidija's with Wendy, who, while serious about her spiritual explorations in Medjugorje, has a light-hearted demeanor that uplifts my more somber nature.

At noon I went to see Father Slavko Barbaric, who often leads the afternoon rosary during the apparition. Soft-spoken and exuding peace, he's one of the most humble and pious people I have ever encountered. "Meet me after rosary at six," he told me in halting English.

At 6:00, I waited and soon he appeared. We walked into the field behind the church, and even though he spoke hesitantly we communicated well. I told him I was easily wounded by harsh words and often felt threatened emotionally, if not physically; he advised that my dreams might be of help. His interest in dreams surprised me, since dream lore has been all but exorcised from traditional religion. I then remembered a dream I had years ago about an unhealthy relationship in which I had been counseled to pray and fast to facilitate healing, and while I tried to fast I had not been spiritually strong enough to do so.

In general, fasting is considered an excellent method for resolving difficulties. Psychologically, it encourages us to dwell on things greater than our earthly desires, while physically, depriving the body of substantial quantities of food gives the digestive system a chance to rest, which in turn promotes keener attunement to spiritual forces. The psychological aspect of fasting, sometimes referred to as "fasting of the heart," requires abstinence from habitual thinking patterns. In retrospect, I'm disappointed that such a remedy, which I still need, must be self-directed, and would much prefer to turn it over to divine intervention. Why does everything have to be so hard? I mutter to myself.

March 28
Tomorrow I am going home. The miracles I have witnessed here have been impressive and moving. Never will I forget the spinning, pulsating sun or the changed rosaries, the energy experienced during apparitions or the radiance on the faces of pilgrims as their hearts were touched by Mary. But even more significant to me personally has been the inner healing I have received, my main purpose for coming to Medjugorje. As a result of this healing, I feel stronger, both mentally and spiritually. Medjugorje, it seems, fortifies a person's coping mechanisms, making it easier to deal with the negativity of the world. And increased freedom from negative preoccupations liberates energy for additional spiritual and material pursuits.

This afternoon I went to take one last look at the church's twin spires and the mountains behind them, remembering my profound emotional release from the laying on of hands. While there, I could feel Mary's love in my heart, easing my pain and bringing me home. Though I have not yet left, already I want to come back to continue my spiritual quest for the goddess among us.

CHAPTER THREE

A Search for Inner Light
Second Pilgrimage to Medjugorje

During my first few months back in the United States, I felt attuned to the spiritual energy at Medjugorje, which had been like a cocoon protecting the delicate new being, with its higher vibration, emerging within me. But the longer I was away from the village, the more I struggled to hold on to the spiritual growth I had gained there. I felt repeatedly thrown back into the negativity of the world—a shock after feeling so spiritually alive. In America there was no spinning, pulsating sun; nor were there crowds of awestruck people with smiles lighting up their faces, or miracles awaiting open hearts and minds. Instead, there were taxi drivers ripping me off, freeway drivers cutting me off, and stressed and irate people everywhere. I soon felt unable to maintain my new sense of being and began losing the motivation to continue my spiritual practices, finding it difficult even to pray.

When I spoke of my experiences at Medjugorje, people were incredulous and either couldn't or didn't want to understand what I told them. If anything, my stories seemed to place an impenetrable wall between us, possibly because they sounded "so Catholic." I now realized with pain that though I could visit the mountaintop I would have to live in the valley.

My resulting condition could not be mistaken for depression or a midlife crisis. Depression was what I had felt *before* going to Medjugorje—a sense of panic and void, of living an unfulfilled life. Medjugorje had lifted the depression and allowed me to experience light and real love. To know such a state existed and not be able to reach it again, caused me anguish, catapulting me into a dark night of the soul. In the chasm of that darkness, I nevertheless had several profoundly spiritual dreams that gave me hope and strength, many containing elements of the miraculous: signs in the sky pointing to miracles, and priests and nuns holding white crucifixes out to me as if urging me to continue my spiritual quest.

Other experiences also encouraged me to keep going. In one meditation, a large white-gloved hand held out a golden ring to me, an image I interpreted as an offer to unite with, or "marry," a spiritual ideal. Upon awaking, I recalled that those who pursue a religious life as a vocation are often referred to as being married to God, while women in religious orders are described as brides of God. The possibility of a closer union with the Divine fostered a conflict in me; a profound commitment to higher ideals might require adjustments likely to produce tensions in my marriage.

Eventually I realized how much more peaceful my dream life was in Medjugorje, no doubt because it was a spiritual haven with less negative energy than the workaday world, allowing for hours of uninterrupted inner work along with the raising of consciousness. My desire to return to Medjugorje became intense; now a prisoner to my moods, I missed the light of higher consciousness I had perceived and knew that my heart was still heavy with unresolved issues. My life seemed hard and difficult this far from the spot I'd come to think of as the "place of the Mother."

Six months after my return, the chance came to go back to Medjugorje, but I was at first anxious. I worried that Medjugorje might disappoint me on the second visit, that the apparitions would no longer be occurring or I would not be open to Mary's energy. Finally, spurred on by the desire to retire my inner demons, I decided to make the trip, and John agreed to join me.

On the eve of our departure I had an important dream:

> There are women standing above me. Next to me is a visionary. Looking up, I see that my head is reflecting the light of the Virgin Mary. Aware that my head shines brightly, I am filled with joy and a prolonged sense of well-being.

The dream seemed to indicate that my second pilgrimage to Medjugorje might entail even greater spiritual growth than the first one, a prediction supported by the following narrative of my trip.

August 10, 1989

Arriving in Medjugorje, I felt as if I had come home again. Perhaps my dark night of the soul is over, I told myself. And indeed, in the center of town the image of Mary greeted me from every corner of the marketplace.

As before, the stalls and stores are stocked with pictures of Mary on medals, posters, T-shirts, and glasses, as well as traditional rosaries and votaries. Although some people seem disturbed by these commercial ventures, they don't interfere in the least with my inner spiritual experience of this place. On the contrary, while examining images of Mary in the stalls, I am reminded of the many similar artifacts and accoutrements associated with early goddesses.

It seems only the dates, locations, and names of the various deities have changed. Archaeological evidence reveals that a wealth of statuary and items such as amulets, coins, and figurines were produced in conjunction with ancient goddess traditions—another reason I am not bothered to find such items at this Marian veneration site.

The rich accoutrements adorning Mary here that also appear in images of early goddesses include crowns, jewels, robes, capes, sashes, and girdles. Such items became significant relics for Christian ritual. For example, St. Thomas was supposed to have received Mary's heavenly girdle, and Christians have been known to pray over various relics of the Virgin's girdle to promote fertility. Again the idea of such parallels intrigues me, and I vow to continue my inquiries about them.

August 11

John and I have settled into the same routine as last March—breakfast, Mass, trek to Podbrdo, lunch, and then afternoon rosary. We share a pension with ten others, including a youth group from Ireland, three couples from the United States, and a young man from Belgium. Our Yugoslavian hosts are pleasant, and over meals we share our plans and the particulars of our lives.

The miracles witnessed by pilgrims recently are as grand as ever, but this is also a still place for inner spiritual development. Without such introspection, the heart cannot be transformed. In fact, although the miracles are impressive and moving, I am slowly becoming convinced that they simply manifest what is happening in the hearts of the people here.

August 13

Coming back was an excellent decision. After a long fallow period of refusing to go inward to deal with my grief, anger, and depression,

I am relieved that the difficult emotional block has lifted and my inner life has been reactivated. I want Medjugorje to stay in me. Also, it thrills me that my husband is here to share this experience again. We are acutely aware of how this place contrasts with our strongly materialistic views, and see our pilgrimage as a welcome opportunity to grow spiritually.

After falling asleep last night, I dreamed of myself in a new role:

> Everything around me and within me tells me ceaselessly that I am a "Priestess for the Most High."

Mesmerized by the dream's promise of love and hope, I felt strongly encouraged to follow my desire to be more than I am and to work for something greater than myself. Though I'm not a bit religious in the traditional sense, and would refuse working for God in any conventional way, the gold fingers of sunlight streaming through the window remind me that this dream is both another reflection of my continuing spiritual growth and an indication that I will receive a better idea of how to dedicate myself to the Divine through my work.

August 14

John and I hiked up Podbrdo early, before the crowds, and had a quiet time of prayer at the outdoor site of the apparitions. The site's power, palpable as ever, is like a current of electricity that I can plug myself into simply by being open. Just sitting on an area of the earth permeated with Mary's energy is enough to ease my tension and open my heart.

As we walked back down the hill, it began to rain so we hailed a taxi. After settling into the backseat of an old car that had stopped for us, we saw a nun walking briskly by and asked her if she wanted to join us. She scooted in beside us appreciatively, telling us her name was Jean. A small woman full of zest, she added, "I've been here for seven months praying for my vocation." This serendipitous encounter made me recall my dream about following a vocation as a priestess.

We arranged to meet Jean at a café after Mass, and as we sat drinking our cappuccinos under the wide canopy that shaded the tables from the Medjugorean sun, I could see that though she was sweet she had inner determination. I told her about the changed rosaries I had seen and asked if any of hers had turned a different color.

"Oh yes," she said, removing three from around her neck for us to see. One had a central silver medallion of Mary, whose heart had turned gold.

"This is so inspiring," I told her. Holding them, I warmed to the energies of awe and love I was sure they were transmitting.

August 16

Over breakfast a couple from California, near the town where I was raised, challenged my view of miracles. "Have you seen the miracles yet?" I asked. "There's an incredible variety of amazing phenomena ranging from the spinning of the sun and color changes of rosaries to the odor of roses from Our Lady, sightings of Mary or Jesus, healings, spinnings and disappearances of the cross atop Mount Krizevac, the illumination of crosses, weeping, moving or bleeding of statues, and signs in the sky, such as significant cloud formations. Photos documenting these phenomena are sometimes passed out."

I could see their bodies stiffen in their chairs as the couple answered, in turn, "Christians should only worship Jesus," then "Medjugorje and Mary are Satan's work."

Although impressed by my firsthand observations of miracles, I knew their real effect was on my inner transformation. So I was saddened that these people, whose Christian views had hardened their hearts against the occurrence of miraculous events, could not use them as stimuli for their own spiritual development regardless of their particular bent.

August 17

John and I met up with Jean for coffee this morning, and she gave me a rosary as a gift, a welcome item as I did not have one. It is made of crushed red rose petals and has a fragrance. Immediately I wondered if it would turn gold. Then, realizing I had gotten caught up in the phenomena here, I reminded myself that it's better to have a miracle of the heart than to see things. Certainly I have had an intense experience of the heart, feeling the strong presence of Mary and the healing of my inner wounds of alienation and loneliness. With this in mind, I am determined to use the rosary from Jean to further nourish my spiritual development.

August 18

Outside the church during a midday apparition, I smelled a thick heady odor but couldn't discern if it was roses. I asked a nun passing by, "Sister, do you recognize that smell? Is it someone's perfume?"

She stood still, stripes of light from the window illuminating her pensive face, then, looking at me brightly, answered, "No, I don't smell anything. Perhaps it's Our Lady manifesting to *you* in this way."

It was a moment rich with mystery and magic.

Later, hundreds of us climbed over the jagged boulders of Podbrdo, holding candles and flashlights to guide our way to another outdoor apparition. The ascent was exquisite, with the candles aglow and everything so quiet we could hear the labored breathing of the people ahead of us, between the occasional "Ave Maria." The pilgrimage up the mountain is as much a part of the worship as the events that subsequently unfold.

Up top, the many pilgrims seeking healing metamorphosed into a throng that pressed toward the visionaries as they stood under the cross. Abruptly the reverent atmosphere of receptivity beneath the stars was interrupted by a flash of cameras and disquieting voices. One man, desperate to touch Our Lady, whom we could hear but not see, pushed through the crowd to stand behind the children and, waving his arms, shouted, "Mother, Mother!" in Italian.

Personally, I am not bothered by Mary's invisibility. I'm content to feel her spirit during apparitions and in personal musings of prayer and meditation. What does bother me is that so many people travel up the mountain for these evening apparitions that they give me less sustenance and peace than they otherwise should.

As I ponder the significance of nighttime apparitions, I observe yet another element connecting these Marianic events to the feminine spirit: they occur in darkness, the domain of the mysterious feminine and of the crone aspect of the goddess. The Chinese image of yin, the feminine spirit, is a dark comma shape with a seed of light embedded within its form. Mary seems like that lighted seed within the mysterious domain of yin's darkness.

August 19

I spent much of the day meditating by myself while up on Podbrdo, in church, and in our room. Taking refuge from my normal routine, I have been reflecting on the insidious effects the limitation of women's roles in society have had on me and others. Women are culturally trained to see themselves primarily as either a mother (madonna) or a sexual being (seductress), and as part of the latter role, to preoccupy themselves with beauty. This perception has led to the cultural distortion of women's true worth and to a predisposition among women to devalue themselves if they do not meet the requisite standards. The ultimate irony is that even women who manage to conform to the limiting roles tend not to feel good about themselves. Women everywhere seem wounded by the struggle to free themselves from the prescribed duties assigned to them by our patriarchal society.

Interestingly, Mary's portrayal by the patriarchy seems to reflect the same limitation of roles and devaluation of power and worth. In particular, her tripartite nature has been hidden and her image desexualized, in contrast to the goddesses of ancient cultures, who were depicted with beautiful bodies and full breasts. In ancient times, virginity and sexuality were not in contradiction, because the term "virgin" had both physical and spiritual connotations; as a result, goddesses were viewed as both sexual beings and virgins. The designation "virgin" was given to temple priestesses and understood to mean unmarried, pure in heart, or in service to the godhead—but with Mary, the term came to mean one who never had sex.

This narrow definition of virginity has kept many women from fully considering the figure of Mary as relevant to our times. In addition, it raised questions among the clergy such as: Did she conceive divinely? And did she have other children by Joseph? The notion of immaculate conception, however, is not unique to Mary. Buddha was born of a virgin mother, as was the mythical Lord Krishna. And Hera, queen of the Greek pantheon of gods and goddesses, was able to generate offspring on her own.

In our times, long after the era of ancient goddess worship, physical virginity often determines a woman's (but not a man's) value, effectively eliminating any remnant of goddess precedents, a limitation reinforced by the Catholic image of Mary as non-sexual—that is, nonpowerful. From this perspective, it becomes clear that the church still claims authority over the reproductive function of women's bodies. One way to take back this authority is by reclaiming the universal feminine aspect of virginity. Mary's virginity is more about purity of heart than a state of physicality. In understanding virginity as being "pure in heart," we might more easily see that Mary functions in the same manner as earlier goddesses, as a universal archetype of the feminine spirit.

After reflecting on gender roles in our society and the conflicts it has caused for women, I took a nap and had the following dream:

> My husband is God the Father. He is on a stage, and three beautiful women approach him. The first woman comes up and abandons herself to him sexually. The next one, who is even more beautiful, also gives herself to him. Finally, the third and most beautiful woman gives herself to him with an intensity I can feel as I watch them. A voice tells me, "The most beautiful is the one who abandons herself to God."

This profoundly sexual dream tells me true beauty is not about how we look but rather about our willingness to devote ourselves to God. The most beautiful individual is the one who abandons herself in service.

As I wondered why the dream's symbolism was so sexual, an answer arose from my body: the intensity of orgasm is often considered the closest a human being can get to physical abandonment. And when the heart is cleansed—that is, "made virginal"—then one can use the activated energies of the body to achieve spiritual abandonment, giving oneself over to the Divine. To me, this dream signifies the importance of rededicating myself to my true life purpose—my spiritual path.

Later in a coffeehouse, I saw two girls beaming while displaying their changed rosaries. One of them, Clare, a fresh-faced girl of twenty who had received her rosary from the visionary Ivan, spoke of her extraordinary experiences in the presence of Mary. As she exhibited her golden rosary, I looked down at my rose-petal one, which still hadn't changed, and felt left out. While admonishing myself for having feelings of self-pity, I flashed on the message of my dream—the most beautiful individual is the one who abandons herself most to the Divine. I then closed my eyes, took a deep breath, and inwardly embraced my life as a gift to be surrendered whether or not I manifested miracles or ever fulfilled either of the two roles culturally defined for women. When I finally comprehended this lesson from my heart, I discovered that my rosary had actually changed: the red petals now bore an iridescent white stripe.

We had dinner at the pension with the Christian couple, who view Marian veneration as "cultish" and pontificate about their concern for what Medjugorje is doing to hurt the church and Jesus.

"If Marian veneration is cultish," I said, "then so is veneration of Jesus *without* Mary." Taking a moment to consider my encounters to date, I realized that Medjugorje did not fit the parameters normally associated with cults. There is no enforced compliance within the group, no dependence on a leader, no need for participants to have money, and no devaluation of outsiders as being bad or wrong. Moreover, Mary is viewed as inseparable from the godhead, and individualized devotion to God is hardly cultish. My relationship with her is personal, I concluded, and does not follow the format associated with cult behavior.

"Venerating Mary just means paying attention to what is happening inside of you as well as outside," I added. "Instead of giving your power to others, you open your heart on a daily basis."

My words fell on deaf ears, however. "We have not searched for answers within," the woman said stiffly. Her husband noted, "We already know that much of what we see here is intellectually wrong." With this, they left the room.

Their dogma saddens me. The real fruits of Medjugorje are peace and love, not dogma and divisiveness. You cannot find spiritual harmony or insight if you refuse to pray, meditate, or at least listen to messages that come from within.

August 20

As I sat with Jean at an outdoor café, I showed her the rosary she had given me, saying, "Look, it it seems to have changed. Don't you agree?"

The nun's eyes lit up. "You're closer to your calling and true purpose," she confirmed.

It comforted me to hear her words, for I saw great strength and courage in her eyes. Her wisdom seemed beyond her years, as if forged in a cauldron of pain. "How did you get to be the way you are?" I asked her.

She laughed and answered, "I lived in a nunnery, where I didn't speak at all for three or four years. That prompted a great deal of profound inner work."

"What put you there?"

She thought for a moment. "I was always called. I have a very deep faith now." For a short time, a shadow seemed to cross her face, but then her ebullient energy surfaced once again. She said simply, "As a child, I was sexually abused by my father for a long time. He warned me I would go to hell if I told, and so I didn't tell. But inside me something hated, and feared, and died. I decided to become a nun to cleanse the pain and heal my wound. I entered the nunnery hating my body, asking God to purify me, to use me. Instead, I was sexually abused by several priests. And like my father, they said not to tell or I would go to hell."

I was shocked. She nodded, saying, "Yes, it was that bad. I asked God to take me, to help me die. I trusted no one. I barely trusted God. How could I, when the very protectors and guides who should have kept his trust for his children were defiling his name by using them for their own secret needs?

"I stayed silent and tormented in the nunnery. I wept and prayed to the Mother. It took years, but she entered my heart. My tears of grief cleansed my hatred."

I felt deep compassion for this courageous soul. She saw it in my eyes and grinned. "It's your own story too, in a different way," she added. "It's every woman's story."

During my time alone, I raged over Jean's account, marveled at her strength, and ultimately agreed with her assessment. Although I personally had not been sexually abused, the abuse of women had turned my mother's initiation to parenthood into a prison sentence. And whereas Jean had become a nun, the title I had been given in my dream was "priestess," a position now extinct, though its male correlate—priest—still exists. In pagan times, specialized priestesses were called nuns; they cared for the sick or dying at healing shrines. By contrast, nuns today, lacking the authority to pronounce absolution or administer sacraments, have had their role effectively reduced to caretaker.

Just last week I witnessed firsthand the church's limitation of the role of women in its ranks. While we were in church before a scheduled apparition, a woman asked the priest on the pulpit, "If Mary is becoming so prominent, does that mean there will eventually be priestesses as well as priests in the church?"

Following a collective gasp, the priest answered in stern voice, "I assure you people, there will be no priestesses."

Hearing this, I determined that although I wish to serve the godhead I refuse to do so merely as someone's caretaker. I am beginning to think my dream indicated not only a yearning for spiritual authority but a desire to be fully valued in a position of serving.

August 21

I recounted Jean's story to John, along with my subsequent thoughts. "If there is ever going to be equality between the sexes," I proposed, "we must address sexism in the church, a major institution responsible for sanctioning discrimination against women."

My husband nodded in agreement. I could see he hoped his understanding might somehow reverse the long history of unfair practices.

I persisted. "Don't you think there should be women clergy in positions equal to those of men and also a nonsexist Bible in widespread usage?"

"It's coming, though I know it's too slow for you," he answered in a tone intended to soothe my frustration.

"Yes, but why should the godhead continue to be referred to as 'him'? How did the masculine ever come to be the sole gender associated with an androgynous source?"

"We're only human. There have been a number of mistakes in our understanding of God," John answered.

"Contrary to what most religious institutions seem to suggest, exclusivity and the intolerance it fosters do not enhance one's experience of the godhead. Since the Divine has given spirit to the world, its interpretation by various religions to substantiate each one as being the only true way is at odds with higher consciousness," I added. "Spirit is nondenominational, but humankind does not understand the principle of one spiritual energy. Mary emphasizes that intolerance and exclusivity are deterrents to a person's spiritual evolution; and it seems important to add that any religion believing itself to be the only correct one thwarts humanity's development."

John assured me, "There is only one Source, which does not practice exclusivity. Everyone is welcome to the banquet. It is human beings who must become less attached to the particular form in which it comes." On this we agreed and shared our hope that such understanding will be more prevalent in the future.

August 22

It is time to go back home. I am sorry to be leaving, because each day of this second pilgrimage to Medjugorje has been pregnant with mystery and heightened awareness of the universal feminine spirit. I've decided to return for a much longer retreat when I can.

Early this morning, before preparing for our departure, I had the following dream:

> I am back at work. My coworkers' faces are menacing. Then suddenly I am in a boat in deep, shark-infested waters, and I am in danger of being eaten up by either the boat's motor or the sharks.

Feeling panic and fear upon waking, I decided this dream was preparing me for something ominous, or even dangerous, ahead. In contrast to my sheltered life of spiritual evolution here at Medjugorje, it seemed to foreshadow conflicts and darkness I might experience in the external world back home. I must brace myself for continuing my inner pilgrimage in the day-to-day world.

CHAPTER FOUR

The Virgin
as a Mother Goddess

This time my transition from Medjugorje to the outer world was different from before, when my emerging spirit seemed as fragile and in need of protection as a chrysalis inside a cocoon. Now I had a stronger sense of my purpose in the world and was psychically and spiritually transformed. The world I reentered, however, was at odds with my focus on spirituality. Although I tried to hold on to my new expansiveness, I felt attacked by friends and coworkers who could not accept the changes I had undergone, and fear enveloped my heart like taut ropes. In the face of such resistance, I began to question if the spiritual transformation I had experienced at Medjugorje was real. Having been trained to ignore my feelings and operate instead from my intellect, I embraced Mary's presence as a path back to my feeling-self and vowed to do everything possible to remain true to my inner life of spirit in the face of this external environment of doubt and denial.

As it turned out, my dreams had indeed prepared me for such trials. For example, I now saw that my dream about deep waters and sharks foreshadowed difficulties I would have in my relationships after returning from Medjugorje. It was hard to prove associations like this through rational inquiry alone, but that did not dampen my enthusiasm for the study of dreams. On the one hand, I viewed them as avenues through which the Divine communicates with individuals, which explained why nearly all religions at some point in their history revered dreams for their wisdom and guidance. Then, too, I regarded dreams as an aspect of the universal feminine principle that encourages within us all an integration of the psyche. In my mind, the prophetic underwater dream announced dilemmas I would have to work through to both deepen my spiritual connection to life and unify aspects of my psyche. It soon became clear that in proceeding along the spiritual path there are increasingly more trials and also more gifts.

I tried to resume as much of a Medjugorean spiritual life as I could. I sat and prayed with the heart, as Mary had suggested, to enable a deep communication. It told me that despite my difficulties my life purpose was becoming more directed.

Then one night I had a curious dream:

> I am in the office of a kindly old dentist I used to work for. I have lost a back molar and am terribly embarrassed. He replaces it with a new one, whereupon I am greatly relieved. "I will work for you from now on," I tell him, "because you have saved me."

In the morning, it was clear to me that the trustworthy gentleman I had worked for earlier in my life personified the spiritual forces healing my childhood wounds. I was gratified by this dream, which suggested that my spiritual unfolding was still occurring beneath the surface of my more mundane preoccupations. Similarly, the lost back molar seemed to represent a situation involving a highly manipulative woman at my workplace, which had been pressing every social strand in my being. As the dream predicted, shortly after my return she suddenly left the office for good and I no longer had to deal with her.

Like my dreams, certain patterns I experienced during and after my visits to Medjugorje were revealing. At Medjugorje, genuine healings took place; back home I fell prey to doubting these occurrences. And when my intellect doubted, my heart felt betrayed. Despite these internal tugs-of-war, however, I was aware that Medjugorje had opened the door to a new way of being and it was up to me to free myself of the "splits" that had produced the initial suffering. Returning home, I concluded, was like retreating to an old consciousness. Unprepared except by my dreams, I had to hold fast to my still-fragile new inner self rather than surrender it to the old patterns of behavior and relationships. What supported me was the knowledge that due to something greater than myself I was no longer working for money or ego but rather for the Divine.

To better comprehend my experiences at Medjugorje and ensure that I would not revert to old patterns, I set myself the task of further investigating the historical, mythological, and spiritual implications of my experiences, beginning with the question of why the feminine energy of Mary evident at Medjugorje affected me so profoundly. Thinking about the spinning sun and the changing rosaries, I became aware that the phenomena related to them extended beyond both Catholicism in particular and dogma in general, and involved an intense energy that could open the hearts of individuals of any faith, as well as those unaffiliated with a centralized faith. The energy seemed more connected to an essence *behind* religion, to the power of the Divine. At first surprised by this realization, I wondered if a Catholic icon such as the Virgin Mary could in fact represent a more universal feminine spiritual energy that might be available to all people regardless of the faith they did or didn't subscribe to.

At this point my research began in earnest. While investigating universal feminine spiritual figures throughout history, I started to discover more and more commonalities between earlier mother-goddess figures and Mary, including the following traits and functions: purity, virginity, intermediary, mother, wife, fertility, healing, protecting, and transformation. The crone qualities of violence and anger reflected in other goddess figures, however, seemed at first hidden in Mary.

In addition to similarities between the traits and functions of Mary and earlier goddesses, it became increasingly apparent to me that the icons and accoutrements associated with Mary were common to various ancient goddesses, as I first noted while in Medjugorje. This seemed to indicate that the Marian symbols were universal expressions of the feminine spirit or archetype.

Perhaps the most visible symbols associated with Mary and earlier goddesses were the numerous celestial elements, which, according to research, had followed feminine deities down through the ages to Mary. Stars, for example, were frequently associated with ancient goddesses. Arianrhod, the Celtic Mother-Goddess, had a silver wheel of stars. Astarte, whom some scholars recognized as a prototype for the Virgin Mary, wore stars in heaven and was called "Queen of the Stars." The name Ishtar, the Babylonian Great Goddess, means "star." And interestingly, the Gnostic name Star of Isis, or Stella Maris, was a title also given to the Virgin Mary. Mary herself is depicted as wearing a robe decorated with stars; having a diadem of stars above her head; or standing on a cloud or crescent moon.

The moon, another universal feminine symbol, was almost always associated with the goddesses of antiquity, and the horns of the crescent moon often indicated power. For example, I was intrigued to discover that the sign of Isis was a crescent moon over a circular disk and the sign for Astarte also included the horns of the crescent moon. A crescent moon was the harvest instrument of the goddess Kore as well, and was at times associated with Diana. Such symbols of antiquity seem to lie at the root of Mary's association with both the crescent and full moon. Perhaps one of the most famous depictions of Mary with the moon under her feet is in the painting entitled *The Immaculate Conception,* by the seventeenth-century artist Diego Velazquez. It is reminiscent of the prophecy of John, who, in Revelation, foretold the new order in these words: "A great wonder in heaven, a woman clothed with the sun, and the moon under her feet, and upon her head a crown of twelve stars" (Revelation 12:1). This woman became identified as Mary as early as the fifth century.

Further, the sun, light, and sky were ancient symbols now sometimes linked to Mary too, although the sun is more frequently connected with Jesus and male deities. In representations, Mary is sometimes depicted as radiating beams of light or a halo, suggestive of the sun's radiance. Mary is often portrayed in the sky, surrounded by clouds, or with clouds under her feet.

I discovered other links as well between aspects of Mary and earlier goddesses. One such link is related to the sea, and the blue of the sea is Mary's color. The ancient name Mari (Mary) in fact meant Mother Sea in antiquity. Likewise, Isis was referred to as the goddess-ship, and her boats, symbols for the womb, were kept in temples. Mary has a similar longstanding association. For instance, yearly, Bayahibe fishermen from the Dominican Republic give thanks to the Virgin by placing her picture in their processional boats.

There are also parallels between animals pictured with Mary and those associated with pagan lore, especially the dove. The dove was originally symbolic of Sophia, the feminine aspect of divine wisdom, and later associated with major goddesses of antiquity, including the Greek Aphrodite. While the dove was originally linked with the feminine aspect of spirit, Christianity subsequently coupled it with the Holy Spirit, the force that impregnated the Virgin Mary; in Velazquez's painting *Coronation of the Virgin*, the dove is portrayed above Mary. And whereas in antiquity the dove is identified with both death and peace, as in Aphrodite's death-goddess aspect called the "Dove of Peace," in Catholic iconography images of doves and statues of Mary often preside over graveyards, and in Medjugorje, Mary introduced herself to the children as the "Queen of Peace."

Another animal connected with both ancient goddesses and Mary is the serpent. The serpent, the primary power animal for many goddesses, was associated with the mother goddess tradition in primitive cultures. In Eastern traditions it symbolized the body's kundalini energy that imparts spiritual wisdom. In Christian tradition, Eve is associated with the serpent in the Garden of Eden. Moreover, authors Anne Baring and Jules Cashford suggest that the biblical Eve is the equivalent of the mother goddess of primitive cultures, whom the patriarchy struggled to dominate. Interestingly, Michelangelo's painting entitled *The Fall* portrays a serpent with a woman's head in the Garden of Eden. Mary herself is often referred to as "the New Eve" by the Catholic Church, where she is depicted as trampling the serpent. Such representations no doubt reflect patriarchal attempts to discount goddess lore and divest feminine spiritual figures of their power.

In addition, my research revealed that lions, cows, and unicorns had been associated both with ancient goddesses and with Mary over the past two thousand years. Historically, lions were powerful totem animals seen beside such goddesses as the Tibetan Tara, Artemis, Cybele, and Lilith. Patriarchal cultures associate the lion more often with male deities and national symbols, which might explain why in Marian imagery it became less common than the dove or serpent.

As for cows, these totem animals of goddesses are often associated with the moon, as seen with the Egyptian goddess Hathor, and the horns of the crescent moon, as an icon of Isis, Astarte, and Kore. In terms of Mary, not only is she depicted with cows in nativity scenes, but the horns of the crescent moon often accompany her, as well.

As I continued discovering the rich mythological and symbolic heritage of the figure of Mary, it became increasingly evident that goddess traits and functions later adapted to Mary seemed to minimize her potential power and authority. For example, long, flowing, and often curly hair was traditionally expressive of the power and sexuality of goddesses; in ancient times, it was believed that women's unbound hair held mystical powers and could control the spirit world. But with the advent of Christianity, the power associated with hair was so universally linked to paganism that St. Paul demanded women's heads be covered. It therefore seems likely that sexual domination played a role in Mary's hair being depicted as veiled, reflecting a movement away from the goddess religions with their emphasis on feminine sexuality, fertility, and power.

Other spiritual symbols associated with the feminine in ancient cultures and later Marian representations include caves, grottoes, and vessels. In primitive cultures, caves were considered wombs of Mother Earth, and thus many goddesses, such as Cybele, had sacred caves associated with them. Similarly, Mary is sometimes depicted as presiding over a cave or grotto; in addition, Jesus was buried in a cave and also born in one where, according to legend, he was nursed by Mary, and so it is called the Milk Grotto. Sacred vessels, perhaps symbolic of the womb, were also originally associated with pagan goddesses. In fact, both pagan goddesses and the Virgin Mary have been called the "Holy Vase." Mary was referred to as "Vas Spirituale" by Christian mystics, and the present-day Litany of Mary addresses her as "Spiritual vessel, Vessel of honor, Singular vessel of devotion." Moreover, Christianity seemingly extended vessel imagery to the chalice and the dish that holds the sacrament and to the retaining bead still found on rosaries.

Another parallel between goddess worship and Marian reverence can be seen in the use of rituals of invocation that were practiced in antiquity and continue to endure. The chants and formulas of goddess traditions can be compared to today's prayers and petitions. Pilgrimages to sacred sites of ancient goddesses for healing are paralleled today by pilgrimages to Marian shrines for healing and divine intervention in human affairs, including those at Lourdes, Fatima, Guadeloupe, and Medjugorje. Many other nurturing and healing qualities universally recognized in antiquity also were later associated with Mary.

The more research I did, the more it appeared that ancient symbols connected with goddesses were reinterpreted in later Christian iconography and linked to Mary. Summarizing the similarities I discovered between ancient goddesses and the Virgin Mary, I came up with the following list:

- Tripartite aspect of the virgin / mother / crone
- Virgin births / immaculate conceptions / divine offspring
- Healing and nurturing functions
- Association with fertility, gardens, groves, and harvests
- Association with disasters and death
- Physical beauty, including long hair
- Queenly accoutrements, such as jewels, robes, capes, crowns, girdles, and thrones

- Titles, such as "Queen of Heaven" and "Our Lady"
- Connected with prophetic declarations
- Invoked through rituals, such as chants, recitations, and petitions
- Honored by processions, festivals, and feasts
- Worshipped at pilgrimage sites of mass veneration
- Symbolically connected to plants and flowers, such as the rose and lily
- Symbolically linked with scents, especially that of rose, lily, and myrrh
- Associated with natural places, such as springs, caves, and grottoes
- Connected with vessels and ships
- Associated with celestial phenomena, such as moon, sun, stars, light, and rainbows
- Connected with the sea, sky, and the color blue
- Associated with specific animals, such as the serpent, dove, cow, lion, and unicorn

Experiential and intellectual inquiry gave me new insight into the heritage of Mary and renewed my sense of purpose. Imbued with a better understanding of the universal feminine spirit, I now felt a sense of historical continuity linking me to people of other times and places. Along with this feeling came the realization of how important it is to regard Mary against the backdrop of earlier goddess traditions so we might reclaim her past, and in doing so, reclaim lost pieces of ourselves.

CHAPTER FIVE

Shadow of the Goddess
Third Pilgrimage to Medjugorje

A long with investigating possible sources of the Virgin Mary's traits, functions, and accoutrements, I began an inquiry into the psychological impact of Marian imagery on people to help me understand why her presence was so powerful. I wondered why pilgrims sought out and were so affected by Marian icons and statues in places like Medjugorje, and why, if the godhead was the essence behind all form, they needed to see her form. I soon discovered that it was because the image of Mary was archetypal.

The Greek root of the word *archetype* means an underlying structure in reality. The twentieth-century psychoanalyst Carl Jung identified certain universal archetypes, or models, that help us make sense of the world, including the Mother, the Father, the Warrior, the Hero and Heroine, and the Wise Man and Wise Woman. Jung believed that archetypes in any society affect its perception of reality and that archetypal images are among the most powerful ways to transform consciousness—more powerful than words, because templates corresponding to archetypes already exist as underlying universal structures in our collective unconscious. Further, he believed that images are powerful because they do not address the intellect but speak directly and symbolically to the deeper intuitive mind. When people respond to Mary, I deduced, they are being affected by the archetypes of the Mother and the universal feminine.

Religions employ many symbols and archetypal figures to take devotees into deeper levels of consciousness and transform them spiritually. Certainly, religious history has documented the transformations of numerous saints and mystics affected by such archetypes, including Teilhard de Chardin, Teresa of Avila, St. Joan, and Bernadette. Transformations of this sort are possible for anyone, and the desire for it is partly what drives millions of people to Medjugorje.

Encounters with archetypal images, as I was discovering on my own, have the potential to bring about lasting changes—in my case, the reversal of deeply rooted negative patterns. When we look at an image of Mary, it is not the object itself that imparts the power but the archetype it represents. Images suggest to our metaphoric mind associations that put us in touch with internal states related to the images, and it is these internal states that transform us. Our deeper, subconscious mind comprehends and reacts to an archetypal presence at the same time that our rational, or conscious, mind cannot understand what is happening.

Because they occur on a subconscious level and their essence is beyond words, it is very difficult to comprehend and articulate these transformations. And while many of the faithful went to Medjugorje to experience miracles but not necessarily translate them into the language of rational consciousness, others, such as myself, struggled to understand the experiences and to bring some of the magic back into our daily lives to share with others. To feel the universal feminine spiritual presence within and share it with others verbally, however, is an enormous challenge. I knew now why many Catholic women I met at Medjugorje could only silently, with radiant faces, transmit, by their presence, evidence that their experiences in Medjugorje had been authentic. Words cannot express the realm of the numinous.

Since people who dwell on archetypal images are linked to the essence behind the form, many people focusing simultaneously on the same form can effect a potential change in the collective consciousness. Dwelling on the archetype of the feminine divine spirit can thus transform negative patterns and create more loving and healing energy in the world. But, I wondered, why had the feminine divine energy come from Mary and why had the visionaries not seen images of Athena, or simply pure light? I concluded that the visionaries probably saw an image of the feminine divine in a form they could comprehend and relate to—one that was culturally compatible and familiar to them. It would be difficult for modern Westerners to have a relationship with Isis, Athena, or any other goddesses removed from our time and culture. While the image of Isis reflected the need for the feminine divine in ancient Egypt, Mary reflects the needs of our times.

Interestingly, Jung recognized the power of archetypal images of the Virgin Mary. After the church had finally officially recognized that Mary as well as Jesus had ascended into heaven, Jung praised the church for this action and considered the elevation of Mary an event of utmost importance for creating equality of gender in society's collective unconscious. While the church refuses to confirm any connection with goddesses of past cultures, Mary's status is slowly being elevated in the direction of equality with Jesus, as evidenced by activity at various veneration sites.

Now I realized why Mary had affected me so much at Medjugorje. In fact, not being Catholic enabled me to see her real intentions behind the rituals and forms, which was to expand our hearts and elevate collective consciousness. If the power of eighteen million people praying to Mary can cause the sun to spin and pulsate, then surely it can alter collective consciousness in our world to bring more peace and healing to people. It doesn't matter if everyone believes exactly the same thing or has the same religious affiliation, only that we are tuned to the same energy. I finally knew without a doubt that Mary was not just Catholic but everyone's goddess.

In addition, the many connections between Mary and ancient goddesses suggested to me that there was continuity between past and present figures of the feminine divine and that this force was manifesting powerfully in our times. They also convinced me that I had spiritual work to do in the world and that my inner work—which would eventually manifest as my outer work—had yet another phase of development to be nurtured at Medjugorje.

During this time of assessing my understanding and future spiritual work, I had a revealing dream:

> I am in a group of people gathered outside, somewhat like a congregation. Beautiful papers in hues of turquoise and pink are being passed out. Their vibrancy fills me with wonder. I am handed so many of them that, while delighted, I don't know quite what I'll do with them all.
>
> Then in the distance I see Mark Thurston, an editor for the Edgar Cayce–based Association for Research and Enlightenment. As the group turns to look behind me, I notice a young girl with auburn hair carrying a cross. She is making her way up front to be crucified. We are all crying, and I feel the intense pain of her crucifixion in my heart.

This dream seemed to be foreshadowing future gifts I might receive by going back to Medjugorje for an extended period of time. But along with those gifts, I realized I might also suffer the pain of life's burdens—my own Gethsemane. Further, the presence of an editor suggested that I wanted the Divine to edit my soul, deleting unnecessary complexities.

I decided to make a third trip to Medjugorje in pursuit of Mary as a goddess. I yearned for additional healing and to accept the challenge of further refining my understanding. The spiritual growth occurring during this pilgrimage was chronicled as follows.

March 11, 1990

I arrived in Medjugorje late tonight, purposely without reservations. It has been exciting to trust the flow of my life in Medjugorje enough not to plan everything. But in the dark, with the now-familiar smell of Yugoslav grape fields in the air, I am tired and want nothing so much as comfort. Since my husband could not spare the time to come, on this visit I am alone, which causes me some anxiety but will also force me to focus more on my inner spiritual work.

March 12

I've managed to find temporary lodgings—a comfortable room near the church. Long-term accommodations have apparently all been reserved by the throngs of pilgrims due to arrive soon for Easter. At least I'm home.

March 14

Today I met a friendly girl from New York, Melanie, who has been living here for two years. A member of one of the visionary prayer groups, she leads healing prayer for people. I like the light and purpose in her eyes, and sense a reluctance to reveal the extent of her experience. I perceive that she is guarding a treasure.

I then frequented my favorite cafés, but scenes once in the foreground—the excitement of the pilgrims and the bustling of the marketplace—have become background, and distinctly uninteresting. It's clear that I am here for a shift that is to be deeper and darker than any before. I can almost hear Medjugorje whispering to me, "I'm going to capture you!"

March 15

I met up with other pilgrims this morning. We climbed Mount Krizevac together and went to Mass. But I had to separate myself from them since they were slow and I had considerable devotional work to do.

I secluded myself in prayer, at church and on Podbrdo, in order to commune with God and Mary to heal my heart. But I sense, too, that Mary as the crone aspect of the goddess will call me into the darkness so that I might also "die" and be resurrected.

I prayed until sleep overtook me, at which point I had a dream:

> It is my birthday, and I am given large dangling heart-shaped diamond earrings. I admire their beauty.

I awoke encouraged by this "birthday dream" that seemed to signify a new beginning. Love—the heart earrings—is being given to me so that I will truly experience it.

I'm beginning to understand the phrase "God *feels* like love." God is a felt sensation in my chest when I pray with intention. Already I feel welcomed back to Medjugorje.

March 16

I woke up to a gray sky with clouds so thick it was impossible to find the spinning sun. The church bell was tolling—a long, ponderous sound, signaling that somebody in the village had died. I bolted upright in bed, listened hard, then began to cry. Over thirty years of grief poured out of me like water bursting from a giant dam. Actually, I've been sad much of the time, lashing out at my unhappy childhood, tired of not knowing who I am, and on most days, estranged from myself.

I'm jealous of mystics who were enlightened in a great flash of illumination. Why can't the Divine take this pain from me right now? It is hard to accept this slow pace of purification and enlightenment.

March 17

I really do feel caught by Medjugorje and hear its voice constantly. "If you're sincere, I'm going to let you see the full magnitude of my power," it tells me. "You're going to experience everything emotionally and spiritually—so much so that what you've experienced intellectually will be pabulum by comparison."

This morning a sudden darkness approached and called my name, triggering an awareness that I am suffering because in the distant past I cut myself off from God. In recent years I have claimed to be spiritual—sitting under pyramids, going to palm readers, studying the occult, reading books about pagan mysteries and goddess traditions—but I am still outside the temple, living a lie, drawn merely to the trappings of spirituality, the fun stuff. Jung says we become whole through encompassing our shadow, the dark side of ourselves. It seems that in the past I strove for this intellectually but not emotionally. Although preoccupied with my pain, I would intellectualize it rather than stay with it long enough for my feelings of distress to be transformed into pure and simple energy. Here in Medjugorje I can safely learn to feel my burdens and, rather than run away from them, free myself to progress spiritually.

To embrace my shadow I must begin exploring the dark elements of the universal feminine as reflected in the crone aspect of the tripartite goddess—the virgin, the mother, and the crone. While the virgin and mother aspects represent the pleasing characteristics of purity, nurturance, and love, the crone part involves the mystery of creation, destruction, death, and war. Integration of these less pleasing emotions ushers in an awareness that enables us to view life in its totality. Finally, emerging whole from this vision, we glean wisdom.

The crone aspect of Mary has never been actively acknowledged by the church, which, by dissociating this tripartite element from Mary, divested her of power. Yet the crone themes remain active in stories of Mary's relationship to death and grief and in images of her waiting for the dying Jesus at the foot of the cross or holding her dead son. The crone element is also palpable in Mary's fifteen promises to those who recite the rosary, which include assurances that the user will be provided for at death. Even materials of the rosary tend to reflect the idea of death. For example, in remote regions of Tibet rosaries are sometimes made from the bone of human skulls; Kali-Ma, in her role as the goddess of destruction, occasionally wears a rosary of skulls; and early Christian rosary beads were at times carved to look like tiny skulls.

Other themes connected with the crone are also apparent in depictions of Mary. Some earlier pagan goddesses were warlike; and as far back as the Babylonian Ishtar, goddesses were associated with aiding victory in war. Mary's association with war is perhaps most apparent when Christian armies of the Middle Ages carried the Virgin's image on their banners as protection. Similarly, earlier goddesses identified with destruction were affiliated with natural disasters such as earthquakes, volcanic eruptions, or tidal waves.

Mary too has issued warnings of destruction to visionaries so they might get humanity to begin focusing on spiritual matters.

Yet another crone element seen within the Marian movement and consistent with earlier traditions is the phenomenon of the Black Virgin. A number of early goddesses were at times depicted as black, including Ceres, Demeter, Melaina, Diana, Isis, Cybele, Artemis, and Kali; modern scholars have associated the color black in these goddess traditions with the earth's fertility. Significantly, Christianity's Black Madonnas, seen throughout France, Poland, and the Americas, are found at sites that were once shrines to pagan goddesses, some of which were subsequently occupied by Roman armies. Many black images of Mary are at pagan shrines formerly dedicated to war and death. It seems the color black represents fertility *and* destruction.

Although knowing the broad range of Mary's functions makes it easier to embrace my own shadow, I was not prepared to greet the many unacknowledged parts of myself that were to spring to visibility in three dreams. The first one I regard as a gift from the crone:

> I am in a show, and I have a beautiful dance to perform but nothing to wear. My father says, "There's your wedding dress. Wear that." I put it on and prepare for my dance in the light, the featured performance because it is for a spiritual purpose. As I am lifted up by another dancer, I bend my body back gracefully and raise my right leg in the air. But when I look down to see who is supporting me, I am shocked to find it's a bitchy girl I've disliked for years, dressed all in black.

Being supported and held up by a bitchy girl dressed in black told me right away that her nature was an integral part of mine and that her negativity was not to be denied but rather embraced as my shadow side. To deny it, I knew, would lead to conflict and internal warring, whereas claiming it could help me integrate my personality. Clearly the crone aspect of Mary is directing me to a place where light and darkness are so unified that I will be able to use these powerful energies in support of each other.

The second dream indicated, much to my surprise, that a union between these two elements, now viewed as inseparable and of equal value, had begun:

> It is nighttime, and a man in black is following me down a dark, narrow alley. I am terrified, but decide to confront him and see what he wants. As I turn to face him, he retreats. I follow him to the end of the alley and emerge into a brightly lit field of flowering trees. Although the man in black is still close by, my fear is gone. We become friends and sing a love song together.

In this dream, the elements of light and dark are once again intertwined but no longer in conflict. The dream seems to represent an emotional and psychological progression in my life.

My third dream illustrated a more advanced integration of the light and dark aspects of my psyche:

> It is dark. I'm tending a garden inside my house, pruning bushes to make them look good. Suddenly, aware that a crippled boy is looking in at me through the window, I lie down and hide in the bushes but soon get up. The crippled boy is now down the hall, and as I approach him, he leaves hurriedly. As he runs

out the door, I close it behind him and call out, "I know who you are. Monkey, monkey, monkey!" He immediately runs back through the door and into my body, where he dissolves until our cells become one. Looking down, I notice that I have no body but rather tiny lights of protoplasm.

The crippled boy in this dream seems to symbolize my unacknowledged emotional and psychological patterns. His dissolution in my body represents the healing that may be possible as I gain consciousness of "crippled" parts of myself that are working below the surface of my conscious life.

All three dreams are surely showing me the crone energy of Mary here in Medjugorje. I am confident that they are helping me confront and integrate the light and dark elements of myself so that I can move forward spiritually.

March 18

Early in the day I had an unusual meditation experience: I became acutely aware of a side-to-side vibration of energy inside me. I attribute these sensations to the goddess energy within me attuning itself to the Source. My conclusion is based on a dream I had two years ago that seemed to foreshadow some type of physical attunement:

I look in awe at the night sky as two beautiful pulsating orbs move toward each other and gradually merge. I recognize one of the orbs as a pituitary gland and understand that soon I will be better able to hear God.

"How long will this take?" I ask.

"Two hundred years," I am told.

I am visibly troubled by the prospect of having to wait such a long time.

"By humankind's time it is long," comes the reply, "but not by God's."

Can it be that the vibratory sensations I felt this morning, I wondered as I opened my eyes, are the result of an anatomical change taking place inside me?

These sensations may in fact represent the awakening of kundalini energy, which in ancient Hindu and Buddhist traditions involves the pituitary gland, often called "the third eye." Kundalini energy, symbolized by a snake, is thought to rise up the spine in two side channels, one representing the sun, or male energy, and the other the moon, or female energy. The side-to-side vibration I felt while meditating correlates with the side-to-side movement of a snake, suggesting a merging of male and female principles, which, physically and metaphysically, enhances spiritual attunement.

It seems my ongoing spiritual practices are contributing to a palpable physical connection with the spirit and a felt experience of the Divine inside me. Just thinking about it stirs a strong sensation of love in the area of my heart.

March 19

What am I living for? Each time I ask myself this question, the answer I hear is, "We are here to love." Then in my imagination I envision all of duality dancing together and forming a vast light of unconditional love. Perhaps this is actually a practice for dying, I tell myself, for welcoming the intense ecstasy that meets us when we leave this world.

I want to learn what ecstasy means. "I love you!" I call out repeatedly, experiencing an influx of positive energy in my chest.

March 22

In church I thought about the mental anguish I suffered through-out my childhood. Feeling a need to forgive those who had hurt me, I prayed and cried.

I have established a routine: Mass first thing in the morning, hitchhiking to Podbrdo for a few hours of prayer or meditation, then home for an afternoon of reading inspirational or metaphysical books. Continuing my spiritual inquiry in this way increasingly assures me that my personal beliefs are being affirmed here, even though they differ significantly from conventional viewpoints. Only by experiencing the Divine directly is it possible to connect with and understand its power.

March 23

I enjoy meeting the long-timers here, some of whom have been in Medjugorje more than two years. For the first time in my life, I feel as though I belong to something—in this case, a secret club that one can join only by searching.

Early this morning I dreamed that something important was about to happen to me:

> I am in a shop where I see two ceramic dolls. Behind their faces I can see gold, which was part of their original castings. I try to pry the gold out of the larger doll, without success. All of a sudden, the gold snaps off her back, and then also off the second doll's back. I am given the gold. I will take it to be forged in a fire, after which it will be returned to me.

Perhaps this dream portends the release of old patterns from my "original mold," or early life, and the "purification by fire."

Maybe my constant fretting will be replaced by a calmness and the awareness of a greater purpose to life. I have asked for this cleansing, and I earnestly desire its gift of transformation.

March 26
Today I followed a strong inclination to observe the spinning, pulsating sun, which continues to confirm my reasons for being here. This time, feeling the sustenance and peace it brings me, I thought I uncovered its purpose: to awaken love in those who view it. The unconditional motherly love I feel in its presence sparks compassion within me.

March 29
At Mass I cried about the fact that my life, now more than half over, has been consumed by emotional burdens. Rarely have I been happy with the people or circumstances in my midst, and lately I have been feeling guilty for having separated myself from God. I see I have a lot of forgiving to do, in terms of both myself and others. Whereas during my earlier visits to Medjugorje I prayed for certain things to happen in my life, now I pray for forgiveness.

On my way out of church I overheard someone say, "The one who has been forgiven has been given everything." I remembered the words of Jesus: "Thy sins be forgiven, and the lame man walked." I too am ready to walk, perhaps for the first time, and am surely in need of direction. I am listening more, awaiting guidance.

For instance, I am acutely aware of the fact that crucifixes have been appearing to me in meditations. Prompted to inquire about their heritage in antiquity, I have found that they were sometimes depicted with a circle through the center, symbolic of the sacred union of masculine and feminine principles. At other times they had solely masculine, if not outright phallic, associations.

Early forms of the crucifix range from the ancient Indian swastika, the Greek cross with equal arms, and the X-shaped cross of Saint Andrew to the Maltese cross of Gnostic origin, the solar cross, and the ansated cross that the early Christians adapted from the Egyptian ankh, or symbol of life. Called the "Cross of Venus," Jung viewed this form as an expression of the feminine principle. Connections between the goddess and the cross occur in Christianity, as in the legend of Empress Helena, the mother of Constantine, who reportedly found the true cross in a crypt under the temple of Aphrodite in Jerusalem. It is becoming increasingly clear to me that religious symbols and traditions as we know them have a heritage in antiquity that is rich with meaning and direction.

April 3

Although I am sure it's been brewing, it seems I'm suddenly obsessed with the idea of leaving Medjugorje. Up until this time I have been able to deal with my emotional tides and psychic turmoil, but today I feel upset and frustrated without understanding why. It's especially perplexing knowing how much growth and peace I have experienced here amidst the pain.

Last night I dreamed the following:

> I am at a cabin I used to go to with my family—a peaceful place out in the woods, away from the world. My girlfriend and I are in the kitchen examining the seed and lime-green flesh of an avocado.
>
> Then I am in the bathroom of my childhood home. Looking in the mirror, I notice I'm wearing thick lime-green eyeliner. I say elatedly into the mirror, "I'm a Jew, I'm a Jew."

Lime green is the color of growth, and seeing it around my eyes reminds me of my third eye, my spiritual center. My association with the term "Jew" is God's chosen people. I conclude from this dream that I, too, am among the chosen and that I now belong.

To me, the chosen are those who attune to the Divine, whether through prayer, meditation, chanting, mantras, Sufi dancing, or any other method of communication. In the past I have worshipped with Muslims, Buddhists, Hindus, and members of various Christian denominations, believing there is spiritual unity among religious followers despite their differing rituals.

April 8

I am again enveloped in an emotional darkness I now associate with the crone aspect of the tripartite goddess. While the virgin and mother aspects are easily assimilated into the psyche, the crone aspect, with its potential for gaining wisdom, has been difficult for me to integrate. What keeps me moving forward through these dark spells are my illuminating experiences here.

One such experience presented itself in an important dream:

> I am in a classroom and God the Father, a male figure I identify as power personified, is sitting up front. As I attune myself with him, he tells me that anything I do in his name through this attunement will be done. The scene changes, and I see my husband about to be attacked. I attune myself to the Divine and, pointing to the light, immediately notice a crucifix there. All of a sudden a big wind comes up, and my husband escapes his aggressors unscathed.

This dream made it seem I was being given direct access to spiritual power for purposes of protecting myself and others, and, when necessary, peacefully confounding enemies to avoid conflict. The Divine appearing in the form of God the Father rather than a female indicates that some forms of protection come under the rubric of male principles. It is good to know I am equipped to protect myself from harmful influences through concentrated prayer and attunement, and that I can call on either male or female principles as needed. This hopeful message has two biblical parallels: the first, from Matt 7:7, "Ask, and it shall be given; seek, and ye shall find; knock, and it shall be opened unto you," and the second, the image of Jesus walking among his enemies without being harmed.

April 15

I am apparently ready to emerge from this latest phase of cavernous darkness. A few days ago I told Melanie that I was looking for someone to pray over me, and she agreed to arrange a session. Today I went to her house, where she and two other women prayed over me. About fifteen minutes into the session I began sobbing soundlessly. The prayer continued, rising in intensity, until my body shook uncontrollably. I dimly understood that terror and fear were leaving my body.

April 16

I wonder if yesterday's cleansing exemplified the snapping of gold from behind the doll's faces in last month's dream. My violent shaking was certainly accompanied by the release of painful unconscious memories dating back possibly to my infancy. So strong were the prayers that Clare, one of the women at the healing, said the heart of Jesus on her rosary began to beat. That, among other things, makes me think Clare is probably being used to conduct a mission in the world.

Clare is another interesting character whose story has moved me. She told me her sister had been violently murdered in Chicago five years earlier. Clare had subsequently lost faith in God and been reluctant to travel to Medjugorje. Arriving nevertheless with her mother and aunt, who had come seeking solace for their loss, she underwent a powerful conversion of heart in response to a series of profound experiences. She explained that during communion the host began to move in her hand, and when she pulled her fingers away it hung in midair. Then the moment she placed the host in her mouth, she began to shake, whereupon her mother and aunt had to physically steady her. Later, when the visionary Ivan invited her up to the apparition room she focused on the wall and suddenly saw Mary's crown. "It looked like a million diamonds," she told me. Clare also saw Mary's hair, veil, cheeks, and a beam of light flowing from Mary's body into her own. Finally, Clare felt the peace she had sought after her sister's death and knew her sister, too, was at peace.

Clare told me the following dream she had had soon after:

> She is in the church at Medjugorje. Ivan has asked Mary if Clare can see her sister, and immediately her sister appears. Startled, Clare asks, "Is that really you?" In response, her sister explains that the visit is a gift from Mary, then she sits down beside Clare in the pew and says that Clare can always talk to her through prayer and that she is happy where she is.

As for Clare's rosary, decorated with a crucifix bearing the dead body of Jesus, though she claims his heart beats on occasion, I myself have not noticed it. I have, however, seen the links change back and forth between silver and gold. Also, the metal on the center medallion has turned pink, seemingly a reflection of Clare's newfound love for life.

April 19

Quite unexpectedly, I was invited to an Easter Sunday luncheon given by some of the expatriates living here. We sat at a long wooden table, with a priest named Father Mark in attendance and Yugoslavs interspersed among people from around the world. Just being in the company of individuals who had communed with Medjugorje's energy for years inspired me. Toward the end of the meal, Father Mark began speaking to each person present about something that has kept them from fully uniting with God. From the expressions on their faces, each listener found his analysis accurate and enlightening. His words to me came as a surprise: he said that although I had known great sadness, God wanted to make my feet dance.

April 20

Through Clare I've been invited to a special prayer group of fifteen people who meet with two girls called locutionists, who hear and speak with Mary *in their hearts*. I am deeply honored to be included.

When we gathered, we knelt for thirty minutes in the soft darkness while each of us took a turn saying the Lord's Prayer aloud. My heart was nearly beating out of my chest, and I was fearful that when my turn came I would forget the well-known words. Then I felt an indescribable spiritual presence in my heart—like a strong night wind full of mystery, Mary came to me. I felt her as a sensation in my heart.

Jelena, one of the locutionists, gave us the message: "Open your sick hearts so that you can become as a light to others who are far from the path." We were assured that the message was not intended for us personally, but for the group as a whole. I know better. I can only hope that I am on the path of developing love and am worthy of the gifts bestowed on me.

April 24

On Good Friday evening, hundreds of pilgrims climbed Mount Krizevac to attend the appearance of Our Lady to Ivan. After reaching the top of the mountain, I was somehow able to situate myself near Ivan, whereupon I knelt and began praying. After some minutes, I knew the apparition had begun because the moonlight revealed that Ivan's eyes had suddenly fixed on something in front of him. Opening myself to the energy, I could feel my spirit being raised within me. The apparition lasted several minutes, and by the time it was over I felt as if I had somehow been elevated.

I now understand why people encountering Mary on this mountain come to think of themselves as beings of light. It turns out that Mary herself told the visionaries that Mount Krizevac could be compared to Mount Tabor in Israel, where the transfiguration, a lighted Jesus, appeared to his disciples.

April 30

I have returned to my job and husband in the United States, but I know that my time in Medjugorje is not finished. On this last visit, while deepening my understanding of Mary I climbed the heights that make the depths easier to endure.

Still, leaving was not easy. As I reached the Yugoslav airport, I felt a pang of sadness knowing the sacredness of Medjugorje would begin to dissipate in the wake of distractions from the mundane world. On the flight home, however, I was sad and happy at the same time, because I understood, like never before, how much the spiritual mother loved me.

CHAPTER SIX

The Goddess Within
Fourth Pilgrimage to Medjugorje

My continuing sense that I was both progressing spiritually during pilgrimages to Medjugorje and having more work to do there kept me focused on an eventual return. My longing to make yet a fourth trip to Medjugorje could hardly have peaked at a worse time, however. The Gulf War was in progress; my husband, independent of these circumstances, was working in Saudi Arabia; and I was anxiously attempting to find out if he was still alive. Once he had managed to get back to the States, and I had broached the subject of my returning to Medjugorje, he was unhappy about the idea, saying the timing was bad and the situation dangerous worldwide. Still, I knew I had to go.

By now fascinated by Marian veneration sites of all sorts, I booked a flight that stopped in Houston, Texas, then rented a car and drove eight hours to visit a Russian Orthodox monastery that housed a weeping icon of Mary. The icon, it turned out, was in a small dark room in the church, cemented to a wall and protected by glass. Tear-stained streaks ran down Mary's cheeks, and her eyes looked moist and sorrowful. Below the icon was a receptacle for catching her tears, into which visitors were allowed to dip cotton so they could touch or taste them. I found her tears sweet. Are they real, I wondered, or were they rigged by clergy eager to be noticed in this remote way-station? It was a fleeting question, for what mattered most to me was the image itself.

Seeing this icon evoked an awareness of how images of Mary served functions unique to the culture they are in. For instance, she is venerated in Montserrat, Spain, as the patroness of married couples and in Macarena, Spain, as the protectress of bullfighters, while elsewhere she is worshipped as a healer. Similarly, her designations in various locales range from "Our Lady of Lourdes," "Our Lady of the Pines," "Our Lady of Gentle Love," "Our Lady of Perpetual Health," "Our Lady of the Prairies," and "Our Lady of Victory" to "Mother of Sorrows" and "The Black Madonna of Czestochowa." I regarded the weeping icon I had come so far to view, and these other cultural images, as outward expressions of Mary. By contrast, I envisioned Mary's archetypal role, geared toward meeting the many demands of popular faith, as an inner expression and the driving force behind my mission to once again dwell in her presence.

After my side trip to Texas, I continued on to Medjugorje. The following narrative describes the inner realizations and continued transformation I experienced in my search for the goddess within.

February 24, 1991

I am back in Medjugorje, and the only lodging available is a tiny, spartan room with a naked lightbulb and no heat. The narrow bed is as austere as a monk's and almost as hard as the floor, a cement slab covered by a thin film of carpeting. The shower stall, a little rectangular cubicle with a shower head aimed off-kilter, will have to do. After all, I am here not for comfort but for inner growth.

And toward that end I am grateful there's a bountiful fruit tree blossoming right outside my window.

March 4
I awake in the mornings to fragrance from the blossoming tree and the weight of my own depression. A *donng . . . donng . . . donng* bellow wafting in through my window tells me a villager has died. The haunting sound reminds me of my own death.

March 15
In this state of deep depression, the only activity I can engage in consistently is prayer. A book I got at the monastery in Texas, entitled *The Way of the Pilgrim*, as well as Mary's injunctions here in Medjugorje, have guided me to pray *with my heart* by putting my attention in the center of my chest, breathing from that space, and then calling out from it. As I do this and focus on my quest for the divine mother within, my depression lifts and I experience an indescribable ecstasy. Each time my entire chest explodes with love, I am nearly overwhelmed by its joyful power.

March 25
Almost daily now, I am having ecstatic experiences, many of which are so blissful I can hardly contain myself. The ecstasy starts as a feeling in my body—an opening in the heart area, like being flooded with light. Oh yes, I tell myself, this is why I've suffered so. But soon the sense of elation recedes and I feel cheated; then it returns, gentler this time. In a sense, the experience of ecstasy in all its intensity entails as much pain as bliss, considering the patience required to accept the slow pace at which it unfolds. This struggle reminds me of the need to embrace my darkness in the effort to find light.

If I had focused only on the phenomenon of miracles—the reports of events that initially drew me to this spot—I would have been impressed but not transformed. I believe my ongoing spiritual transformation has resulted from my willingness to embrace personal darkness, which has introduced me unexpectedly to its counterpart, ecstasy.

March 27

My purpose for living has gradually been revealed to me through encounters with the darkness of the crone, the purification of the virgin, and now the love of the mother. For me, the mother's unconditional love is the most healing aspect of Mary, but it was necessary to experience the crone and the virgin as well to achieve clarity and embark on the path of genuine spiritual growth.

I now know I am to serve the goddess not as a nun but as an ordinary person bringing spirit into the secular world. I am to behold Mary as a goddess with a heritage that goes back to her ancient roots. I am to do my part to bring Mary's energy into the world, to make a place in society for all aspects of the feminine so others may experience her fullness and power too. I also know that if we use Mary's power correctly—not to hurt others, but to access and comprehend our own divine nature—peace will come into our hearts and upon the land.

The wars raging in cultures throughout the world intimate that it is time to expand our view of the feminine until the image becomes internalized and universal. For then more people can be nourished, healed, and guided to find their purpose and their peace.

CHAPTER SEVEN

Lessons from the Goddess

Returning home this time, I could not avoid the fact that the Divine is manifesting in Medjugorje in an unprecedented way. The miracles occurring there provide a deep feeling that one is on a walk with the goddess. But more important than the site's miracles is its potential for promoting emotional and psychological healing.

For me, experiencing the Divine through *feelings* has been the most compelling and ultimately transformative lesson derived from my encounters there. Although an absence of feelings does not correlate with absence of the Divine, feelings, particularly ecstasy, form the matrix of an inner knowing that convinces us even in nonecstatic moments that something powerful is happening.

It is said in orthodox circles, however, that you "cannot go on feelings." Dreams, visions, channeling, and hearing God's voice are all at times discredited. In addition, the church considers anything related to astrology or the occult suspect; yet the Bible is full of such elements, including signs from the heavens seen by the three wise men over the place of Jesus's birth. People who anguish over "proper" criteria of a legitimate spiritual experience can easily be led astray by sanctions imposed by the church or any other faith-based organization that uses social pressure to instill standards of acceptability. For one thing, following spiritual awakenings such individuals may come to discount their genuine experiences. For another, they may refrain from sharing them with others, fearing condemnation and ridicule.

To foster greater spiritual evolution in the world, it is necessary to put more faith in our spiritual experiences. The fact is, that in spite of the reluctance some people have about sharing their spiritual encounters, increasing numbers of individuals around the world are experiencing the Divine directly. Faith and acknowledgment are the touchstones for evolving spiritually in today's world. The goddess shrines of the past must have had a similar intensity of purpose: to unite humanity with the Divine.

The second lesson I learned from being in the presence of Mary at Medjugorje was the significance of praying with the heart rather than with words and intellect. Her teachings made it clear to me that prayer can be even more effective when the individual focuses on the *physical* center of the chest and makes sincere invocations and requests from this area.

The practice of opening and purifying the heart has roots in antiquity. Egyptologists point out that in ancient Egypt the heart was considered the center of the self, the physical place where the soul resides in the body. Various goddesses were believed to take possession of people's hearts, sometimes even eating them or swallowing them. In a parallel fashion, Marian messages at Medjugorje encouraging pilgrims to focus on the heart include the following, which were recorded in a brochure entitled *Mary's Message to the Visionaries* and later compiled in a book authored by "Medjugorje" and called *Messages to the World from the Mother of God*. Here Mary admonishes her followers to "Give me your hearts" (May 15, 1986), "Abandon your heart to me" (December 26, 1985), "Open your hearts" (May 23, 1985), and "Change your hearts so they can be like mine" (May 15, 1986).

When I first began to pray with my heart in Medjugorje, the ecstasy I felt entailed physical sensations that were indescribable. The sensations turned out to be part of a purification that enabled me to feel great love in this area of my body and in my life. Such an outcome may have been a response to my requests to feel more love in my life. Or it might have been stimulated by a deep bonding with Mary's message "You know that I love you and that I am burning out of love for you" (November 20, 1986).

A third lesson I learned from my encounters with the goddess was the importance of pilgrimage. While pilgrimage can be an inner journey to greater understanding and enlightenment, it is an age-old custom to journey outwardly to power spots as well. Along with the well-known religious sites of Marian visitations, other sites inspiring connection with the Divine include the Great Pyramid, Stonehenge, Borobubdur, Mecca, and the Dome of the Rock. Numerous shrines from all religions honor specific places as having sacred energy. From time to time certain individuals also incarnate with this power, such as Jesus, Buddha, Muhammad, and numerous female deities.

Both historically and today, it is believed that the energy experienced at sacred sites, also known as power places, can catalyze rapid spiritual evolution. And the trigger is not only the site but the pilgrimage leading to it, particularly when undertaken in a state of openness and desire for spiritual growth. It is in large measure because of pilgrimage that power places like Medjugorje end up positively influencing the world and transforming the consciousness of pilgrims who visit them.

The many long-term effects from my experiences include a stronger relationship with creative forces and the Divine, more patience and greater love for others, a more balanced personality now virtually free of depression, a more positive outlook with less focus on negative occurrences, and a spiritually directed career that has given me a new purpose in life—working for an unseen source. Along the way, the figure of Mary as goddess has helped me rediscover and reactivate the feminine within myself, which now serves as a vital link to other cultures and continues on as a wellspring of personal wisdom and strength.

CHAPTER EIGHT

The Living Goddess

Mother of divine grace, pray for us
Mother most pure, pray for us
Mother most amiable, pray for us
Mother most admirable, pray for us...*Virgin* most powerful, pray
for us
Virgin most merciful, pray for us
Virgin most faithful, pray for us...
Mirror of *justice*, pray for us
Seat of *wisdom*, pray for us
Cause of our *joy*, pray for us...

—Excerpted from Litany of the Blessed Virgin Mary

As a result of my pilgrimages to Medjugorje and my investigations in comparative religion, I believe it is possible to view Mary as a mother goddess for the modern age of transformation. By adding her to the recognized lineage of mother-goddess figures—Inanna, Ishtar, Astarte, Isis, Cybele, Artemis, and Athena—we extend the continuum of the feminine archetype in the West from the most ancient times to the present. Simultaneously, we reintroduce into acceptability the shared attributes of mother-hood, purity, virginity, intercession, wifehood, fertility, healing, protection, violence, and anger. By viewing Mary as a mother goddess with universal significance, we not only broaden our view of her capacities but also make her accessible and relevant to people of all cultures, thereby fostering unity among them.

One such attribute, though it is often overlooked, is breast-feeding. Examples of breast-feeding goddesses date back to the Babylonian Ishtar, the Egyptian Hathor and Isis, and the Greek Hera and Artemis. In fact, the constellations and the Milky Way were thought to be made from the breast milk of Hera, the Queen of Heaven; and Artemis (Diana), known for her numerous breasts, was the patroness of nurturing, as the famous statue of her at Ephesus testifies. Like these ancient goddesses, Mary was portrayed baring her breasts, suckling, and at times exuding milk. The church, however, later considered such imagery "inappropriate" for the Mother of God, and hence these depictions fell out of popularity.

Although Mary as we know her today has seemingly been cut off from her historical roots, if we are willing to put aside rigid doctrines and dogma and understand in our hearts all that she represents, we will have laid the groundwork for reintegrating the feminine principle into our consciousness and feeling a new sense of wholeness and harmony—or what has historically been called a new order. John the Evangelist is said to have been referring to a new order, an age of body-mind healing that many people feel is presently manifesting, when, in describing "the New Jerusalem," he wrote: "A great and wondrous sign appeared in heaven: a woman clothed with the sun, with the moon under her feet, and a crown of twelve stars on her head" (Revelation 12:1). The fact that John portrayed this new order as an unidentifiable woman suggests he associated it with an ascendancy of the feminine principle. The crown of precious gems that form the foundation of his New Jerusalem—jasper, sapphire, emerald, topaz, chalcedony, sardonyx, sardius, chrysolyte, beryl, chrysosprasus, jacinth, and amethyst—represents emblems of goddesses since antiquity; jewels in general, according to Jung, are metaphors for wholeness within the psyche. But while the feminine principle has often been correlated with wholeness, the church rapidly identified the woman of John's vision as Mary, perhaps to prevent worshippers from making outside associations.

Followers of Eastern thought also believe that a new order will be brought about by an increase of feminine energies, and predict that that the ancient mother will awaken once again to sit rejuvenated on her throne, bringing peace and benediction. According to an ancient Hindu idea, the Great Mother will destroy the present universe in the last world age, as a result of humanity's failure to perceive deity in the feminine principle, and that an increase in crime, violence, and the breakdown of society signals the approach of this end-time.

Indeed, it appears that if we do not heed Mother Earth's warning signs to rebalance our male-dominated viewpoint, the outcome might be destructive for our culture. We can perhaps see Mary's visitations and messages at veneration sites such as Medjugorje as efforts to help raise the consciousness of humanity to meet this challenge. The resurgence of the universal feminine principle is reminding us that it is time to nurture ourselves and the earth before it's too late.

The phenomena occurring in Medjugorje dramatize the ideas taking root around the globe. Everywhere, it seems, events are fostering a change in consciousness, motivating us to gain awareness of past perspectives, achieve insight into ways to lead a balanced life, and understand the need for all humanity to collaborate as stewards of the earth. This we can do by moving toward a balance so our society is neither matriarchal nor patriarchal, but integrated. Our task is therefore to let go of erroneous boundaries and preconceived notions of feminine and masculine, and realize that both elements are necessary to healthy functioning and progression toward higher consciousness. Once this shift is made internally, the necessary changes in religious and societal structures will follow.

This age of mind-body healing foretold in earlier times was said to bring masculine and feminine forces into balance and in some respects pointed the way toward this unification. The Gnostic Gospels, for example, foreshadowed the coming of such a balance in the expression "Mother-Father God." Today we might think of this new worldview as a "Mother-Father reunion." And for this reunion to occur, Mary must become viewed as spiritually equal to her male counterpart, Jesus. Despite avid Marian veneration at sacred sites such as Medjugorje, equal reverence has not been sanctioned by the church. As early as the fourth century, according to *The Panarion of Epiphanius of Salamis*, the Bishop of Salamis (ca. 315–403) made negative references to women who worshipped Mary by offering cakes to her, a customary practice reminiscent of goddess worship. Worshipping Mary was seen as a threat to the patriarchy's insistence on exclusive devotion to Jesus—so much so that theologians are still careful to define acceptable avenues for her veneration. Nevertheless, veneration of Mary and the practice of invoking her aid became widespread, and to this day devotees request her intercession as the ever Virgin Mother (an appellation reflecting church dogma), "Co-Redemptrix" (an epithet not officially accepted by the church), or even the third member of the divine Trinity identified as Father, Son, and Virgin Mother (a designation the church considers heretical).

Apart from the church's official views, lay devotion seems to suggest equality. And one long-standing popular religious belief—

held for nearly two thousand years before becoming officially sanctioned—was finally acknowledged when the Roman Catholic Church decreed in 1950 that "Mary was taken up body and soul into the glory of heaven." Many paintings and descriptions also portray this elevated position of the Virgin. For instance, in the painting *Coronation of the Virgin* by Agnolo Gaddi, Mary is seen as both Jesus's bride and his mirror image, symbolically suggesting the equality of the two aspects of divinity: male and female. Other artwork shows papal devotion to Mary. A fresco commissioned by Pope Calixtus II (ca. 1119–1124) in the Chapel of St. Nicholas, in Rome's St. John Lateran, portrays Mary enthroned alone, without Jesus, above two popes, while other representations depict popes in prostration clasping her feet. Such images, amplifying the power of Mary's position in the church, are important seeds of change.

Should we object to Mary because she is Catholic? Not at all; rather, let us remember that goddesses from other times were identified with specific religions and, more often than not, served patriarchy. It seems more than coincidental that an increase in societal acceptance of women as equals has coincided with an increase in visitations of Mary around the globe. Although many feminists may disagree with this view due to their perception that Mary as a Catholic deity is a puppet under patriarchal control, I believe that the movement toward acceptance of women in society is directly related to veneration of Mary and Marian apparitions as she is our most evident feminine symbol.

Eventually, we must see Mary and her son, Jesus, as equal aspects of one energy, something the early Gnostics foreshadowed when they prayed to "Mother-Father God." That energy, known also as the Divine, is ultimately an androgynous source that radiates intense love. And while this Source has no labels or religious systems, we have created human images to represent it, such as

Buddha, Shiva, Mary, Muhammad, and Jesus. Yet when we look beyond the multitude of labels and forms, we encounter energy from the light and love of which they are composed.

Medjugorje is about transcending physicality and moving toward that light and love. The new consciousness it births, awakening genderless perceptions of the Divine, coalesced for me in a dream I had toward the end of my fourth and final pilgrimage there:

> I am in the upstairs bedroom of my home. I have been asleep but suddenly awaken to notice that the rosary I am holding in my left hand has turned from dark brown to pink, a pigment that is now leaching out all the way up my arm. Pulsing with love, I run to show my husband my arm then dash out to the balcony. The view across the stairwell reveals that a new room has been added to our home, and an immense orb of magnificent light is speaking to me. It is conveying a message of intense love and an awareness that it holds within itself infinite forms. I fall to my knees in awe, and as the orb leaves I cry for its return.

Now, mere recollections of this dream remind me that the goddess is living. Sometimes she appears as an innocent virgin, and at other times like a knowing crone. Most often she comes as a mother gazing lovingly upon her child or cradling the earth itself. Having felt her presence in Medjugorje, encountering her in my dreams was not surprising. What took my breath away, however, was later to find her living in my heart. From her crèche in human hearts around the world, this mother goddess can teach us to embrace our oneness, individually and collectively, as we inch our way toward peace and understanding.

In Praise of the Living Goddess

Hail! Holy Queen! Mother of Mercy,
Our life, our sweetness and our hope.
To thee do we cry, banished children of Eve.
To thee do we send up our sighs, mourning
and weeping in this vale of tears.
Turn then, O most gracious advocate,
Thine eyes of mercy toward us.
And after this, our exile, show unto us
the blessed fruit of thy womb.
O Clement! O Loving! O Sweet Virgin Mary!
Pray for us, O Holy Mother of God
That we may be worthy of the promises of Creation.

Glossary

Archetype. A model or prototype; a term coined by Carl Jung to describe universal models that characterize the collective unconscious of humanity.

Attunement. Communion; the act of aligning oneself with and harmonizing with divine vibrations.

Chanting. A method of communicating with the Divine, both internally and externally, through the creation of sounds.

Father. A term used by patriarchal societies to describe the most supreme being, or godhead; an anthropomorphic designation that ascribes a gender to the Divine.

God. Male archetype of the Divine, personified in the West as Jesus; indivisible energy comprised of both male and female aspects; synonymous with the terms "creative force," "godhead," "Supreme Being," "cosmic consciousness," and "the Divine."

Goddess. Feminine archetype of the Divine; originates in mother goddess traditions of primitive cultures.

Godhead. Highest or supreme power of the universe; synonymous with the terms "creative force," "God," "Supreme Being," "cosmic consciousness," and "the Divine."

Kundalini. According to ancient East Indian belief, spiritual energy coiled at the base of the spine and, when awakened, interactive with the chakras, or spinning centers of energy along the spine; energy traveling from the base of the spine to the head, often redistributed back through the body.

Locutionist. A person, often a religious mystic, who communicates with internalized archetypal principles.

Meditation. A spiritual practice used for invoking and communicating with the Divine and for gaining increased awareness of the self and the godhead.

Odor of sanctity. A strong pungent smell, often of rose, lily, or myrrh, associated with the presence of the Divine; manifestation of the Divine in the physical realm in the form of a scent.

Our Lady. Epithet for the Virgin Mary; a term used for numerous goddesses of antiquity.

Patriarchy. A system of social organization based on succession through the male line, in which the dominant authority is held by men.

Pituitary gland. An endocrine gland attached to the base of the vertebrate brain, emitting secretions that affect other endocrine glands; according to ancient East Indian belief, the third, or inner, eye of wisdom and universal oneness.

Power spots. Places where people feel intense divine energy, such as the Great Pyramid, Stonehenge, Borobudur, Mecca, Dome of the Rock, and numerous other outdoor or indoor religious sites.

Prayer. A spiritual practice used to invoke the Divine either internally or externally; a means for internalizing spiritual forces.

Rosary. Beads used to recite series of prayers in the Roman Catholic Church for purposes of spiritual communion; devotional beads used in other religions, such as Islam and Hinduism.

Visionary. A person who serves as a channel through which the Divine communicates with humanity.

Selected Bibliography

Bacovicin, Helen, and Walter J. Ciszek. *The Way of a Pilgrim.* New York: Doubleday, 1979.

Baring, Anne, and Jules Cashford. *The Myth of the Goddess.* New York: Penguin, 1991.

Begg, Ian. *The Cult of the Black Virgin.* London, UK: Penguin, 1985.

Berger, Pamela. *The Goddess Obscured.* Boston: Beacon Press, 1985.

Bolen, Jean Shinoda. *Goddesses in Everywoman.* New York: Harper & Row, 1985.

Brunton, Paul. *A Search in Secret India.* York Beach, ME: Samuel Weiser, 1989.

Cavendish, Richard. *Man, Myth and Magic.* New York: Marshall Cavendish, 1970.

De Montfort, Saint Louis. *True Devotion to Mary.* Rockford, IL: Tan Books, 1989.

Eliade, Mircea. *The Encyclopedia of Religion.* Chicago: Chicago University Press, 1988.

Gadon, Elinor W. *The Once and Future Goddess.* San Francisco: Harper & Row, 1989.

Giles, Mary E. *The Feminist Mystic.* New York: Crossroad, 1982.

Hoffman, Glyna-Lee. *The Secret Dowry of Eve.* Rochester, VT: Park Street Press, 2003.

Johnson, Buffie. *Lady of the Beasts.* San Francisco: Harper, 1988.

Jung, Carl. *Archetypes and the Collective Unconscious.* The Collected Works of C. G. Jung, vol. 9. Princeton, NJ: Princeton University Press, 1980.

Kinsley, David R. *The Goddesses' Mirror.* New York: State University of New York Press, 1989.

Livingstone, G. "Motherhood Mythology." Unpublished thesis. Berkeley, CA: Graduate Theological Union, 1981.

Medjugorje. *Messages to the World from the Mother of God.* League City, TX: CMJ Marian Publishers, 1997.

Michell, John. *The Earth Spirit.* New York: Crossroad, 1975.

Monaghan, Patricia. *The Book of Goddesses and Heroines.* New York: Dutton, 1981.

Neumann, Erich. *The Great Mother.* Princeton, NJ: Princeton University Press, 1974.

Nicholson, Shirley. *The Goddess Re-Awakening.* Wheaton, IL: Theosophical Publishing House, 1989.

Olson, Carl. *The Book of the Goddess.* New York: Crossroad, 1990.

Pirani, Alix. *The Absent Mother.* London, UK: Mandala, 1991.

Preston, James J. *Mother Worship.* Chapel Hill, NC: University of North Carolina Press, 1982.

Roberts, Alison. *Hathor Rising.* Rochester, VT: Inner Traditions, 1997.

Ruether, Rosemary Radford. *Womanguides.* Boston: Beacon Press, 1985.

Sjoo, Monica, and Barbara Mor. *The Great Cosmic Mother.* San Francisco: Harper & Row, 1987.

Starbird, Margaret. *The Goddess in the Gospels.* Santa Fe, NM: Bear & Company, 1998.

Stone, Merlin. *When God Was a Woman.* New York: Harcourt Brace Jovanovich, 1976.

Swan, James. *Sacred Places.* Santa Fe, NM: Bear & Company, 1990.

Walker, Barbara, G. *The Crone.* San Francisco: Harper & Row, 1985.

Walker, Barbara G. *The Woman's Encyclopedia of Myths and Secrets.* San Francisco: Harper & Row, 1983.

Walker, Barbara G. *Women's Rituals*. San Francisco: Harper & Row, 1990.

Warner, Marina. *Alone of All Her Sex*. New York: Vintage Books, 1983.

Wilshire, Donna. *Virgin Mother Crone*. Berkeley, CA: Ten Speed Press, 1990.

Witmont, E. *Return of the Goddess*. New York: Crossroad, 1982.

Zimdars-Swartz, Sandra L. *Encountering Mary*. New York: Avon, 1992.

About the Author

Judith T. Lambert commutes between worlds. For twenty-five years, she has divided her time between an international community in the Kingdom of Saudi Arabia and a home in the San Francisco Bay Area of California.

Judith holds a master's degree in Religious Studies from John F. Kennedy University in Orinda, California. Extensive travels enable her to deepen her study of cultures, languages, and religions firsthand.

She lives with her husband, John, and their daughter, Gabrielle. Her other books include *Gabrielle's Magical Pets*—a picture book illustrated by Gabrielle—and *The Light: A Modern-Day Journey for Peace*.

ORDER FORM

Quantity   **Amount**

_____ *A Mother Goddess for Our Times:*
Mary's Appearances at Medjugorje ($14.95)   _____

Sales tax of 7.7% for New Mexico residents   _____

Shipping and handling ($5.00 for first book;
$2.00 for each additional book)   _____

Total amount enclosed   _____
Quantity discounts available

Method of payment

❏ Check or money order enclosed (payable to Ann Duran
   Productions in US funds only)
❏ MasterCard ❏ VISA

CREDIT CARD #: _____ EXP: _____

Ship to (please print):

NAME _____

ADDRESS _____

CIT/STATE/ZIP _____

PHONE _____

ANN DURAN
PRODUCTIONS

1704B Llano Street #239, Santa Fe, NM 87505
Phone: 001-966-3-878-1811
www.annduranproductions.com